# Vine Stories:
# How an App Changed Our Lives

By Jennifer Dent
and Yolanda Baker

*Illustrations by Mike Bennett*
*Cover graphic design by Bryan Thompson*

## *Foreword*

## *@James Helm*

Originally from the UK, I have lived in Australia for the past nine years, and lived in Los Angeles for three years before that. I am a father, actor, writer, producer, and fool. I have an Honors degree in Film, Television, and Media, and I have worked in so many different types of jobs that if you name one, I've probably done it somewhere along the line.

When I discovered Vine, I was staying at a friend's place (a fellow Viner) in the US. The app had been around for a few months, and as with lots of things, it was more popular and widespread in the States than in Australia. I thought it was great fun, but I wasn't sure what I would post. After all, my phone was old with an awful camera. I watched vines for a few weeks before I attempted my first post, which was a display of how much I dislike chopping onions, and it wasn't great.

First, (like other social media sites such as Facebook and Twitter) it was just a way to stay connected with faraway friends and amuse myself when I was bored. When I suddenly began to get comments and "likes" on my posts, I realized that there was a whole world of people just like me out there using the app, not just minor celebrities trying to get exposure.

It was amazing to see what people were creating and supporting on Vine and they inspired me to do more of my own. When a funny idea struck, I would shoot and post it. The two greatest things about Vine are that it has limitations (which I believe inspires creativity) and that it is instant. Within a minute or so of the idea forming in my brain and my posting it, the vine is out there in the world for everyone to see.

When I started vining, I think I might have given some people the wrong idea about why I used the app. My non-Vine acquaintances believed I was trying to get attention, gain professional exposure, or that I was doing it out of vanity. If you watch any of my vines, you will realize that this is clearly not the case. I have had real life friends unfollow me on other apps when I have informed them that their opinions of what I should be doing on my own profile were of no concern to me.

I saw the true value and potential of Vine. It is an all-encompassing community of loving, supportive people. Of course, there are always going to be hacks, showoffs, idiots, and trolls, but that's the way the world of social media works. Vine represents the world as a microcosm in your hands. It reminds you to never judge a book by its cover. It shows you that brilliance, creativity, love and support can come in infinite shapes, sizes, ages, and colors.

I realize many people on the outside just see Vine as some silly little app, but for many people it is a life-changing support system. I count myself as a member of that community.

People are dealing with many issues in their life, such as bereavement, divorce, disability, illness, depression, anxiety, or just plain loneliness. Knowing that there is a whole community of people on Vine who are there for comfort, support, and practical advice means more to me than I can express, I doubt the original designers of the app could ever have envisioned the attachment and engagement that Vine allows us.

Vine restores my faith in humanity. I may sound like a creative type with thin skin and exposed emotions, however, I have suffered depression, often made worse by losing faith in mankind as I watch the world get more corrupted and the wrong people continually "win".

Vine reminds me that I am not the only one who thinks this way and that the world is still populated with caring, open-minded, talented, intelligent human beings. I cannot put a price on how much Vine has improved my mental state and my outlook on the world. I belly laugh more times a day than I can ever remember doing before.

The connection I feel with my Vine community and family can't be measured. I will probably never meet most of them in real life, but I will never be able to thank them enough for the positive effect they have had on my life. There are many who I know I will remain lifelong friends with, possibly even marry, and for that, I am forever grateful.

## Preface
### By Yolanda Baker

I'm a voracious reader and I've been writing for pleasure since I was ten. I'm an accountant who helps the disabled with their healthcare costs and the author of three (somewhat dry) books on medical expense tax deductions.

Jen and I are not professional therapists or medical experts. Although Jen is a nurse, there is no advice that she offers in this book. Simply, we are two old (according to Vine's demographics) social media users who realize that the way the Westernized world expresses emotions is changing.

We appreciate everyone who agreed to take part in this book. To those whose stories that we were unable to publish in this book, know that we are grateful for the time you've given us. We are developing a website, www.yourVinestory.com, and we are expanding it to include the stories that we did not include in this book.

We are indebted to our families and friends who have supported us through this project. We would also like to extend a special thank you to Andrea Bedard for her time and effort in helping us streamline this compilation.

*Please note: Any information in this book is not to be taken as medical, legal, tax, or other professional advice. Please seek the advice of a professional for any medical, legal, or financial problems.*

# *A Quick Tutorial on Vine*

Here are words and phrases that may not make sense if you are not familiar with Vine.

Vine:  A social media application used by iPhone and Android users to show six seconds (or less) of video.

Viner:  A user of the social media application, Vine.

Hash Tag (#):  One word or a combination of words that becomes a searchable Vine link, which organizes topics. Users can search a hash tag to find all of the vines that have been placed in that category in the "Explore" section.

Post (or Vine Post):  A six second (or less) video uploaded onto the Vine application from a Viner's account.

At Symbol (@):  Used before a Viner's username to allow messages or replies to be sent to that user on Vine.

# SÉANCE

I THOUGHT I WAS TOO OLD TO MAKE NEW FRIENDS
NOW GROWN UP AND MOVED ON FROM SO MANY,
BUT LOOK WHAT HAPPENS WHEN FOLLOWING TRENDS
WADING THROUGH BULLSHIT THAT'S TEN A PENNY;
A DARK-HAIRED RIP I FOUND WITHIN THE TIDE
SHUNNING LOW HUNG FRUITS FOR JEWELS HIGHER UP.
A BRUISED BUT HAPPY SOUL, SHE WOULD NOT HIDE,
USING TALENT TO DRAIN A RICHER CUP
ENOUGH BULLSHIT, LET'S BE FRANK: YOU MADE ME
LAUGH AND THAT WAS HARD TO DO AT THE TIME
OVER TWO THOUSAND MILES YOU MADE ME SEE
SOMETHING IN MYSELF, THAT YOU MADE ME VINE.
   I WONDER ON YOUR SCENT AS WE'VE NOT MET
   A GHOST FOR A FRIEND AND I LOVE YOU YET.

*Leo Cookman*

*Poem Courtesy of @Leo Cookman*

# One

## Love Found

## *@Christiawna and @Rory_Eblen*

### *"Thaw"*

I downloaded Vine in May of 2013. I knew of the app's existence for some time before I signed up, but hadn't really been interested in exploring what it was. I guess it was something about the then recent ex-boyfriend signing up for it that triggered that human reaction of not wanting to be the last one to participate. If he was going to have an account, you better believe I was going to have one. Username: Christiana. Simple enough. I watched the tutorial; I made my first vine. *Hey, this is pretty cool.*

Let's be honest, my "vining" wasn't all that good at first. Some short clips of a drink disappearing from a glass or my friends and I being nutty on a Monday night in Central Massachusetts were the extent of my "six second films." But a month or so passed and I quickly grew into my "characters." I started fun hash tags. I joined the Late Night Party Patrol (a random group of silly night owls who danced and acted in front of their phones, often until the sun came up, always hoping they didn't wake the neighbors.) I interacted with strangers across the globe daily. I found myself in the middle of an amazing community I could have never imagined. It was wild. I liked these people. They liked me. **I liked me**, and I was so busy pumping out one liners and dancing until 5 am that I had forgotten to be sad about that ex. Vine wasn't just a creative outlet; it was a sort of therapy for me. Little did I know there was so much more on the horizon.

It was summer, sometime in June/early July, and there was this one guy following me who tagged me in a bunch of original six second songs. He was part of LNPP. He participated in my tags. He liked my singing and wanted me to do some song collabs (a popular trend of playing someone else's vine while singing/playing music over it and filming your own vine.) *Who is this Rory Eblen guy? He wants me to sing over these songs? He tagged me in **another** vine. I'll check him out.* Rory was pretty cool, so I followed him. "I might be in Boston soon, we should make vines!" The New Yorker said. *Nice.*

After a few more weeks of daytime vining and late night dancing and character acting, I realized the combination of the inconsistency of my work schedule and my late night Vine antics were taking a toll on my brain. I was exhausted, out of balance, and neglecting daily responsibilities. My main issue was that I hated my job and needed to find a new one. Things were rolling together into a perfect storm and I was overwhelmed, so I decided to take a couple of weeks off from Vine so I could balance things out. It was July 29th. I announced my break to my Vine followers and the outpour of support and love was overwhelming. I cried. I vined it. More support and love followed. I received two messages via Twitter.
One of them was from Rory:

"Hope all is well! Just wanted to say that you're awesome

and to never forget it! Stay strong and hope to see you in the future."

I thanked him; told him I just needed some time to straighten my life out and clear my head, etc. We innocently exchanged phone numbers in case the opportunity arose for some in-person Vine collabs, and then we began to chat a bit. We discussed music, nature, and art. I just happened to have a piece of art I made that featured music and nature, so I sent him a photo. I felt something.

We've communicated every day since that afternoon.

The image of Rory walking toward me on the day that we finally met outside of our phones is still burned in my brain. It was during the wee hours of a cool August morning. It was dark. I picked him up at Union Station in Worcester, Massachusetts, about forty minutes from where I was living. He was wearing a maroon hoodie with a bear on it and tan cut-off shorts. His hair was long and his face was full of life. I took him to a local diner where I sat nervously in my red sweater, avoiding eye contact and nursing a hot mug of coffee and a glass of water. After the diner, we sat on a bench overlooking the Quinsigamond Lake in a somewhat failed attempt to watch the sun rise thanks to the trees. His arm was around my shoulders and I was nestled close to him, this stranger from the internet. "Hey, I wanna tell you something." He whispered, shifting as if about to share some secret. I obligingly turned. He kissed me. We spent three genuinely amazing days together.

Today is March 5th, 2014. I'm writing this from a small bungalow on eastern Long Island. That art piece is on the wall. His drums rest quietly in the office. Both of our names are on the lease. Over the course of seven months, we've shared our story on Vine, starting from the first day we met to just last night when Rory was making dinner and dancing in our kitchen. We laugh, we act, we make music, we capture raw, genuine moments. Our vines are the moving photo album of our unexpectedly beautiful pairing. It hasn't all been sunshine and candy, mind you. Long distance is hard work. It takes dedication, commitment, and patience (*What patience?*)

Missing each other, not being able to see each other conveniently, was tough. "Wait for the thaw." Rory would say, always focused on our spring plans to move in together, always encouraging me to look toward the future. One thing is for sure: sitting alone in my car for four hours during the routine 200 mile car rides wasn't always enjoyable, but it was always worth it.

Some say Vine is "just an app." I strongly beg to differ. It hasn't even been a year since I created my account and my whole world has changed in so many ways, for the better. It's pretty wild. If it weren't for this powerful little app there would be no story; there would be no **us**. Rory would have continued to play his music and ride his bike around Long Beach, completely unaware of my existence, and I would have continued to pair music and nature on canvas in Massachusetts, totally unaware of his. Instead, here I sit in the house we share with a heart packed full of gratitude and love, constantly thanking the Universe for this amazing person I get to spend my days with. In my nearly 28 years on this earth (this past year being my most concrete proof) I can tell you two things I know to be 100% true: you can find love in the most unconventional and surprising places, and our worlds can shift and change at any given moment. I don't know what paths life will take me down next, but you can bet one hand will be on my phone, Vining each adventure. The other hand will be holding on to Rory's.

## @*Ameera Belle* and @*Ben Talley*

My best friend showed me Vine in my San Francisco apartment. We scrolled through the app for hours that night as she shared her favorite Viners with me. The next day, I created a profile. My first, and mainly all the vines I posted for months, were silly little videos of the babies I took care of. They weren't very creative; just babies being cute. I used Vine as more of an observer for months until relocation placed me in Los Angeles. My life then began to shift into the beautiful creation it is now.

When I moved to LA, the need to create began to consume me. I began to experiment with darker stories as well as comedy. Through my poor attempt at comedy, I found a group of late night Viners, one of them was a young, rambunctious guy by the name of Ben Talley, and he instantly caught my attention.

On a warm October night, I was visiting my family in San Diego. I was bored out of my mind, watching Netflix and scrolling through my Vine feed. The late night Viners were just beginning their silly antics, and I once again saw that same interesting person, Ben Talley. I wondered, "Hmm…how else can I check out this weird but entertaining guy?" The answer was Twitter. I "favorited" more of his Tweets than I can remember that night.

Not long afterwards, I received a direct message from him. "STALKER," is all he said. I was a bit unsure how to respond to that message, but I rolled with it and replied with some joking, witty response, and it worked. We began messaging back and forth. My heart was racing. I could not believe I was talking to the person with whom I had been so intrigued by for quite some time. After private messaging for a while, we exchanged numbers. We then texted well past sunrise telling each other our life stories, our dreams, our struggles, and everything between.

We video chatted later, after barely sleeping for a few hours. Seeing his lips move with the simultaneous sound of his voice was captivating. Up until this point, I had only seen six-second clips of his comedic persona through Vine. What I was seeing on that video chat was an entirely different person: A real side of Ben Talley. One I never dreamed I would experience.

Throughout the next month, we talked daily. Any moment I had free was spent with him, electronically. He was on the east coast, freezing in his cavernous apartment while I was on the other, over heating in the California sun. During one of our nightly conversations, we discussed the fact that a few Viners were coming to LA for a meet up. I didn't expect him to make it all the way out to California on such short notice, but what he told me next made my heart skip a beat: he was coming to the Vine meet up. I was in shock. I was going to see him in real life. I would be able to see his oddly long and slender face with those giant alien eyes right in front of me.

The day he flew in I drove to the airport to pick him up. I swear I had to have lost ten pounds just in nervous sweating on the way. I parked my car, found his baggage claim, and waited. I could have thrown up from the anxiety. People began walking through the doors, and I kept my eyes peeled for the mysterious Ben Talley.

How tall was he? What kind of clothes did he wear? Would he recognize me? Would I recognize him? The moment he walked through that door, I immediately knew it was him. We made eye contact, a huge smile filled my face, and then we hugged. The energy in that hug was filled with nervous energy, but mostly happiness. That week was one of the greatest and most overwhelming weeks of my life. When he left to go home, we were different.

For over a month, we fell asleep every single night together on video chat, only ever hanging up when I needed to work. Our bond was stronger than ever and the pull to be physically together again was getting more difficult to resist. What were we going to do? He hated Los Angeles and would never move there. He lived in Virginia, and I wouldn't move there. When Ben told me that he had decided to move to New York City, I had my answer. Within two weeks of Ben moving to the city, I packed my little car with the belongings I cared about and drove 3,000 miles across the country so that we could finally live a life together.

Things are sometimes still difficult, but that's expected. I have days when I wonder, "what the hell am I doing?" I'm sure Ben has the same. The difference is that we are here together. We can take those moments of doubt and insecurity and help each other push through and find our peace. Ben is my wild card and I will continue betting on us until the end of time.

*"Everything is alive so that I can be alive:*
*Without moving I can see it all:*
*In your life I see everything that lives."* - Pablo Neruda

## *@Tony Tomahawk and @Chelsea Tomahawk*

Vine is a medium in which I can express my general disdain for other humans. When I first discovered Vine, my intent was to use it as a little window into my nihilistic brain. If you were to look back at my original, long-ago-deleted vines, you would find six-second clips of me hitting myself in the face repeatedly, slamming my head against solid surfaces, or enthusiastically vomiting. Soon enough, I began to interact with surprisingly like-minded people on the app. I began to see it as a way to connect with other bored, alienated weirdos.

I first interacted with the fiery vixen known as Chelsea What somewhat shortly after I'd gained a small following. We formed a quick friendship through Vine. I've always favored Viners with few followers and bad attitudes over the highly popular ones with their tired shticks. Chelsea was quick-witted and also the damn sexiest lady I'd ever laid my astigmatized eyes upon. It's difficult to tell what a person is really like from six-second videos, but I felt unusually drawn to her Italian appearance and her sense of humor. Pretty much, I had a crush on a girl in my phone. I happily discovered that we both lived in southeast Michigan.

Eventually, Chelsea contacted me and let me know she'd be in my area that weekend. I told her that I would meet with her and her friends to make vines. It was a cool feeling, but still a little nerve-wracking considering I had never before met anyone from Vine, let alone anyone who even knew what Vine was.

We met at a lavish "Gay Christmas in July" party thrown by her friends. I will always remember the first time I ever saw Chelsea, standing in a back alley behind the apartment in a red dress, texting. She looked so good that it seemed heroic. The party itself was awesome, equipped with an open bar and a Gay Santa handing out swag-bags. I violated my probation with a few drinks to take the edge off, and soon enough Chelsea and I were hitting it off like old friends. We had some slightly sloppy heart to hearts at a few gay bars after the party died down, and from the first time we hugged to the first time we kissed I felt like serendipity had accidentally mistaken me for someone who was more deserving of good things.

The next morning, Chelsea convinced me to ride back to her city and spend more time together at her house. I was hesitant, but ultimately I did. We began spending more and more time with one another, not to make vines anymore but just to be together. I took a Greyhound bus to see her every week. We got matching tattoos of each other's initials on our ring fingers. We fell in love with each other, and it fucking ruled. Chelsea asked me to move in, and I did. Every day with her is a great one. We've become so close that we joke we're almost one person.

Recently, we moved into a new apartment with a shared lease. The wood floors are awesome. We have two cats, and a legendary canine named Rambo. I plan to marry this girl. If I had never downloaded Vine – if *Chelsea* had never downloaded Vine – none of this would have happened. I'd still be living at home, unemployed, kind of irritable, and maybe just a little lonely. Thankfully that's not what happened. Vine changed my life in a major way, by bringing me together with my partner for life. And that is cool.

*Two*

Family and Friends

## @Paulette Griswold

12/24/12, 8:10:32 PM - 8:10:38 PM: My sister-in-law proclaims her love for me at the Christmas Eve gathering with that "bit-too-much-to-drink" glimmer in her eye, then turns and asks why Matt (my husband) is so quiet tonight.


12/25/12, 4:22:15 AM - 4:22:21 AM: I march around the house in a frenzy, collecting Matt's belongings. I'm no longer giving him a choice; he hasn't slept in over 50 hours. When you can't walk up the stairs because breathing is too hard, it's time to go to the ER, regardless of your holiday plans.


12/25/12, 8:45:01 AM - 8:45:07 AM: I'm waiting for Matt's mother to pick up the phone so I can let her know we will be late for Christmas breakfast because her son is receiving blood transfusions. His BP is through the roof, fluid is gathered around his lungs, he's severely anemic and on the verge of a stroke, but I won't be able to tell her why.

12/26/12, 2:07:56 PM - 2:08:02 PM: It feels like there's no air in the empty waiting room, just pressure folding down and upon me from all directions. I try to focus on the TV in the corner. Matt is in the procedure room a few doors down having a catheter inserted into his jugular vein for emergency dialysis. A man passing by in the hall asks if I'm okay.

12/28/12, 4:11:23 PM - 4:11:29 PM: I'm walking next to a rolling bed again as we make our way to another painful procedure. The monotonous web of hospital hallways becomes a fitting symbol for the unrelenting fear that's boxing me in and steering my every move.

12/30/12, 5:35:41 PM - 5:35:47 PM: My dad hugs me as I explain that my strong, fit, always-healthy husband is being tested for cancer, AIDS, autoimmune disorders, viral infections, and diseases I've never even heard of, and the results will determine whether the kidney damage is permanent. I've given this news a dozen times, but this is the first time I give it with tears.

1/8/13, 2:31:36 PM - 2:31:42 PM: After copying another set of readings into my "kidney binder," I snap it shut and place it on my hip like a toddler. I look around for my keys so I can warm the car before driving Matt to his first in-center dialysis treatment.

2/1/13, 7:13:22 PM - 7:13:28 PM: I'm staring at the blank "Name" field for a new Facebook page. Out loud, I suggest "Kickass Kidney for Matt?" He laughs.

3/23/13, 8:42:26 PM - 8:42:32 PM: Our bed wobbles as Matt twists in pain because a plastic tube is sucking on the lining of his abdominal cavity. My back is turned to him. I pull up the covers and let my tears dampen the pillow in silence.

4/7/13, 7:06:14 AM - 7:06:20 AM: I open my eyes and sink into the warm relief of waking up from a bad dream. A few seconds go by, and then I hear it: the hum and swish of Matt's home dialysis machine. Reality shoots into my pounding heart and wraps me in a cold sweat. I wonder when I will stop waking up this way.

4/26/13, 4:13:55 PM - 4:14:02 PM: Matt is napping again, so I'm running. Every time my foot hits the pavement, I'm pounding out thoughts. "This isn't fair." "This is impossible." "The best days of our lives might be over." I pound them away, leaving them behind me and reaching forward, chasing after the notion that we will get through this, one day at a time. One step at a time, one minute at a time, things will get better. I try to believe it.

5/21/13, 10:12:57 AM - 10:13:03 AM: I'm watching an adorably goofy video text from my cousin. It looks as though she has filmed and edited it on her phone. I begin typing back, "How did you do that?"

5/23/13, 3:48:09 PM - 3:48:15 PM: The project manager & I are in the middle of our office filming each other jumping in the air and giggling at ourselves. We're trying to remake a vine of some guy named Rudy Mancuso hovering in the air.

6/2/13, 5:50:48 PM - 5:50:54 PM: Matt is napping and I'm cooking dinner. I decide to make my first "comedy" vine called "#drunkcooking." I realize I've laughed more in the past week than I have in months.

6/18/13, 1:06:34 PM - 1:06:40 PM: I hit a record high in "likes" on a vine I just posted of my cute outfit, as the camera pans down to my dog shitting beside my feet. I can't believe strangers are calling me funny.

7/10/13, 7:12:14 AM - 7:12:20 AM: On the way to work, I am parked on the side of the road wearing a huge rainbow clown wig. One hand is holding a phone up in the air; the other is flipping up the middle finger.

7/10/13, 9:21:53 AM - 9:21:59 AM: I get a notification that Christiawna, a Viner I admire, revined #crazyclowndrivers. I do a happy dance at my desk.

7/23/13, 10:19:42 AM - 10:19:48 AM: Still unsuccessful in our search for a kidney donor, I have decided to utilize my latest social media discovery. In my car where I have privacy, I make a simple vine stating that my husband needs a kidney and requesting visits to our Facebook page.

7/23/13, 7:02:35 PM - 7:02:41 PM: Matt's jaw drops in disbelief as I tell him that over 3,000 people have revined my announcement.

7/24/13, 4:16:24 PM - 4:26:30 PM: I am walking down a street in the middle of a busy town square wearing a pink clown wig and carrying a bouquet of plastic flowers. I am about to meet someone from Vine in person for the first time. I press the screen to record as I round the corner and see Christiawna and Ryan sitting at a cafe table.

7/24/13, 8:33:21 PM - 8:33:27 PM: Matt and I are sitting on our bed scrolling through endless "#KickassKidney4Matt" vines made by strangers across the nation and beyond. Someone named Tony Oswald had asked for a kidney in a fast food drive-thru. We just sit and laugh and say "wow" over and over.

7/28/13, 4:32:41 PM - 4:32:47 PM: I'm wearing an old woman's hat and making a joke about UK Viner Leo Cookman and the royal baby for my first ever #vinehack. I realize this is the first time all year that I've gone a whole week without crying, besides the happy kind.

7/30/13, 6:57:23 PM - 6:57:29 PM: I'm using a red dry erase marker on a white tank top, filling in a black outline copy of the "Kickass Kidney" superhero created by a Viner named Jon Carter. Pressing the marker into the fabric, I shake my head back and forth with a huge grin on my face.

8/19/13, 11:57:33 PM - 11:57:39 PM: I'm writing "LNPP" across my face with eyeliner. It's my first time participating in a group Vine challenge with nightly hash tags run by Tony Oswald. I'm supposed to be finishing my work, but it's a welcome break from a toiling all-nighter.

8/22/13, 10:42:30 AM - 10:42:36 AM: I pause my work to check Vine and squint at a page full of new notifications. Chico Bronson noticed me vining my grief earlier that morning and had started #makepaulettesdaybetter immediately. People I didn't even know were participating. It worked.

9/1/13, 5:11:45 PM - 5:11:51 PM: The dry erase marker is out again. I'm drawing a face on an upside-down pot so I can remake a Bollywood lip sync vine by MR DAVIS. I place the pot on my head in the mirror and laugh so hard it falls off. Matt doesn't have to ask what I'm doing.

9/18/13, 9:33:34 AM - 9:33:40 AM: I'm sitting at the airport with Matt reading supportive comments on my vine about flying with his dialysis equipment for the first time ever. I feel as though the world is cheering for us.

10/5/13, 11:23:41 AM - 11:23:47 AM: I'm considering a hash tag for a looping vine of myself dancing with my dog. I realize I'm addicted to looping, and that dancing always makes the day better. #dailydancewithpaulette is born.

10/23/13, 8:38:12 PM - 8:38:18 PM: I am wearing a surgical mask and expressing the miracle of dialysis through dance to the sound of Ben Talley's vine in which he plays "You Sexy Thing" on the guitar. I wonder if I've ever had this much fun alone, and decide that no, I haven't.

12/18/13, 5:47:12 PM - 5:47:18 PM: I'm talking to Matt about how much I want to meet more Viners in person. He repeats a suggestion he's made earlier: "Why not invite them all here?"

12/23/13, 6:41:12 PM - 6:41:18 PM: I had been dreading the approaching holiday because it would mark a year of living with kidney failure, but some of our best friends are staying in the house with us and the urge has hit. I have set up my phone and iPod dock on the mantle, I am handing out Santa hats and they know exactly what's coming. I can't resist a Henry The Fifth #cantdancechristmas loop.

1/17/14, 11:33:21 AM - 11:33:27 AM: My birthday is already so good that it makes up for the previous year. Every time I check my phone, there's a new #pgBdayBlitz vine from another great person. I decide to stay in my pajamas and vine all morning.

1/23/14, 10:54:21 PM - 10:54:27 PM: I'm outside the airport terminal approaching two people known to me as BigOsaBaller and NamesTooCommon. I've been wondering all week whether I'm crazy, but follow I my instincts and give them each a huge hug.

1/25/14, 9:48:11 PM - 9:48:17 PM: The last of my 26 guests have arrived and most of them are gathered in my kitchen. I'm quietly letting it all soak in. Everywhere I look; there are sleeping bags, beer cans, phone chargers, and faces of people I feel as though I've known my entire life.


1/26/14, 12:20:41 AM - 12:20:47 AM: Time slows down for a minute as I walk the upstairs hall of my usually empty ten-room colonial. I pause in the middle and slowly turn, realizing that there is a vine happening in every room of my house. Every vine is about finding a kidney for my husband. I feel a pulse of collective energy buzzing around me, a hot wire of inspiration shooting through every gesture of affection and triumph, popping in cheers and cracking in laughter. I take another step and realize that something big-- something incredible is happening, and it's happening to us...six seconds at a time.

# @ScrambyEggs

Vine is unlike anything I have ever experienced with social media. I first heard about Vine from comedian Patton Oswalt. According to Patton, Will Sasso was performing skits on the app, and if we weren't watching, we were missing out. After witnessing a few of the now-classic "Lemon" vines by Sasso as well as several vines from Marlo Meekins, James Urbaniak, Steve Agee, and Adam Goldberg, I was hooked.

I started out recording simple, silly vines. I was afraid to show my face, but as I started to gain a few followers, I realized that my creativity was entertaining other people. In turn, their creativity inspired me.

I felt ready to finally put my own face in a vine after I watched several posts from a hash tag called #mein6. Those vines were quick biographies of the Viners who were participating in the hash tag. The vines were simple, honest, and powerful. This Vine theme showed people's hearts and humanity. I wanted to participate, so I made a silly vine in which I said, "Me in six spins in my messy office" while spinning around.

Later, I made a vine about having sleep apnea. During a sleep study, I stopped breathing twenty five times in one hour. Before that night on Vine, I was embarrassed about my condition. It is often mistakenly thought of as being a condition amongst the morbidly obese. My sleep apnea vine received a response bigger than I could have ever imagined. Several people commented that they too, had sleep apnea, or had loved ones who had it. I was amazed at the level of positivity I received. No one was calling me names, telling me that I had a problem, or expressing apathy toward my condition. I truly felt unconditional love and support from my Vine friends.

Having newfound confidence, I eventually joined the "Vine Hero Game", created by @Hey Kitty. The game grew from brainstorming sessions, an organic experience that evolved along with the app and the participants involved. My character, "ScientistSyd" began as a bumbling assistant (mostly designed for comic relief) and later evolved into a major character who has some real issues. It has been a once in a lifetime experience of which I am proud to be a part.

Someone commented on one of my vines, "Your posts bring me joy. I like many Viners, many make me laugh or in awe of their creativity, but few bring me joy… and that's a talent. Those other things are fleeting; joy isn't forgotten". I took a screenshot of that comment and a handful of others and saved them. They honestly floored me.

To know that simple, six-second looping videos I posted were making other people happy was a tremendous thrill for me. I have gained several followers since I began in March of 2013, although certainly not enough to be considered "Vine famous" by any stretch of the imagination. Follower counts don't matter. It's the connections shared through Vine, even between two people that matter.

I have had the pleasure to meet and share creative ideas with many of the friends I've met through Vine. They have given me so much more in terms of friendship and support than I ever could have imagined. These are friendships that I am confident will last a very long time, despite the geographic distances.

As a newborn, my daughter, Bella, always slept in one particular position. The bones of an infant are soft and easily distorted, and the skull is not yet fully formed. At about three months of age, she developed a flat spot on her head. The doctor recommended a different sleeping position for six months. No matter how hard I tried to keep her from doing so, she always ended up in the same sleeping position. I tried all sorts of ways to keep her from lying that way, none of which worked. I suffered from extreme sleep deprivation during those six months, staying awake to constantly monitor and reposition her.

After the six-month period ended, the spot on Bella's head was still severely misshapen. The doctor recommended that we visit a pediatric cranial specialist who diagnosed positional plagiocephaly. The specialist told me that it would not improve on its own, and that she needed a customized helmet to help form her skull back to its normal position as soon as possible. He told me that after the age of a year and a half, a baby's skull begins to fuse together. If the helmet was not used before that time, she would have to wear it until she was twenty-one years old. She was already nine months old, and we were running out of time.

We submitted our claim to our health insurance plan who kept us waiting for a month, only to deny it. I appealed the denial, calling the insurance, specialist, and the helmet company. When the appeal came back a month and a half later, it was once again denied. The helmet was supposed to cost $5,000 out of pocket, but I negotiated with the insurance and the helmet company and they decreased the price to $2,500.

I didn't have the money. I asked my family for help but they were not able to assist me. It was just after Christmas and we were almost out of time. Bella was about to turn one year old and the helmet would take a month to create. After that, it would take six months to begin treating Bella's positional plagiocephaly. I felt hopeless and helpless.

I turned to Vine for help. I only had about 1,500 followers, and needed to get everyone's attention. I made a vine holding up cue cards that I had written on about Bella's condition. I didn't think anyone would see it, much less respond to it. I was wrong.

The post exploded. People I didn't even know donated. Some contributed only a few dollars, but anything helped. We met our goal in just two days. A few of my family members did end up contributing, but Viners gave us most of the funds needed in order to get the helmet.

Bella is no longer disfigured, and it's all because of Vine. My little girl was saved because strangers wanted to help her. I can never be thankful enough. My faith in humanity is restored.

# @GENE

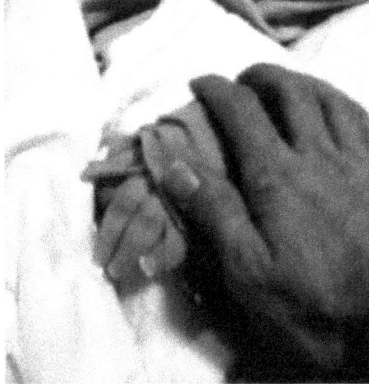

As I'm writing this, it has been less than a month since I lost my wife to cancer. I have used Vine to externalize what I was feeling inside and to show what I was experiencing, but I was selective in what I wanted to show. My posts were bits and pieces of the experience, but it was enough to show people what was going on.

The vines of my wife in the hospital are the most emotionally charged vines I've ever done or probably ever will do again. My current vines don't get the same support from people that those did, and that's fine. I'm not too worried about the number of "likes" or followers I receive. Vine is a tool for expression. I'm not trying to be some sort of Vine superstar. I'm not trying to be popular.

The saddest vine for me is the post from January 9, 2014 in which I am holding my wife's hand in the hospital. It makes me tear up just thinking about it. It's very sad.

I regret that I didn't take a lot of pictures of us together. I have a few pictures of us on her iPhone, but that's all.

If anything, I hope my experience has taught people that they are not alone. If you're going through grief, take it to social media and talk about it. You might find it to be therapeutic. You also may discover that there are a lot more people who care about you than you realized. Give it a chance.

As a memorial to my late wife, I'm leaving that Vine account open, but I will no longer be posting vines in it. You can now find me at @g_e_n_e.

# Three

# Comedians

# @Mike Gambino

*Originally from Chicago, Mike is an actor, standup comic, improviser and writer living in Los Angeles, California.*

Chicago, 1996. I was with a friend parked in front of a grocery store. I had to run in for some essentials. Being the class clown, I used to do this trick where I'd kick the bottom of a door while simultaneously moving my head back to create the illusion that I walked head first into the door. I noticed my friend was watching me walk up to the store so I figured I'd freak him out, only this time, I had the bright idea to do this trick off the large display window in the front of the store. I ran up, and due to a horrific miscalculation, I kicked the bottom corner of the window where it met the brick inlay. The window spider-webbed and I attempted to regain my balance by putting my hands out, but my arms broke through the glass and a large shard came crashing down, slicing my left wrist all the way through the medial artery.

In shock, I ran back to my car screaming, "We gotta go! I just busted out that window!" I actually opened the door with that hand, hopped in and sped off. One block later, my hand went limp and slid off the steering wheel. I slammed on the brakes, and without putting the car in park, my friend and I got out of the car and switched seats. He raced me to the hospital.

As a result of my brilliant idea, I almost lost my hand that night. By law, doctors are only required to chop it off and stop the bleeding. Fortunately, the doctor took my age into consideration. "I figured you're probably going to need this thing for awhile," he said. It took six and a half hours of microscopic surgery to save it, but today, I have full range of motion and a scar. More than half of my hand feels like it is asleep, but I'll take it, because if I had chosen to wait for an ambulance, you wouldn't be reading this.

I thank God for that accident.

During my rehabilitation time, something wonderful happened. I turned into an asshole. I moped around asking my dad for a few bucks everyday so I could buy weed, cigarettes, and malt liquor. My girlfriend at the time gave me an ultimatum, "Figure it out or I'm gone. I don't like who you've become." She suggested I write a list of ten things I enjoy doing, so I did. Number one on the list was "watching movies". She said, "Instead of watching movies why don't you try being in them?" I signed up for an acting class, fell in love with it and never looked back.

Today, most of my time is spent running from audition to audition, writing jokes for my stand up, shooting a TV episode or doing improv with one of my two comedy teams, *Lunchbox* and *Socially Attractive*. In between all of this, vining!

Vine has become like a second family to me, as I'm sure it has for many others. You learn from and make friends with people from all over the world, gazing at a series of six-second snippets into their life.

I know Viners who have asked for our votes because they're on a televised reality show. I know Viners whose content pushes the limits of our understanding within the confines of the app itself. I know Viners who have spontaneously cracked up laughing at the ridiculousness of what they're doing. I know Viners who have fallen in love, and I know Viners who have broken down and cried.

When I see somebody reaching out to the Vine community asking for help or asking to keep a loved one in prayers, I think back to that accident. I think about the people who saved me. Although I may be a thousand miles away, I try to be there for those people. You never know if your vine or your comment is the difference between life and death. It may give somebody that extra push to give tomorrow a shot.

There's a Viner whose sister is terminally ill. Every day, she visits her sister in the hospital and shows her my vines. She says they make her laugh, even though sometimes it hurts to. That's amazing to me. I would never have thought that some little phone app could do something so incredible. The Vine community has the power of prayer. The Vine community has the power of listening. The Vine community has the power to heal.

Strangers helping strangers: something this world could use a little more of.

## @Alx James

Before Vine, my life was completely different. I wanted to play sports, and I was very involved in volleyball. It practically consumed my life. At the time, I guess you could say that it was the love of my life. Everything I did revolved around the game. All my friends were from volleyball. Eventually, I ended up getting hurt and, on top of that, I had an argument with my team and didn't go to the last game. I was lost. I didn't know what I would do.

I auditioned for American Idol and made it to the Hollywood week twice. I got sick both times and couldn't continue the process. It was heartbreaking, and I was left, yet again, trying to figure out what to do next. I was a vet technician in North Carolina. I also did some modeling and was an extra in a few productions taking place in the area, but I didn't really get any satisfaction from it. I kept telling myself that there was something missing. I always knew that I wanted to entertain people. More than that, I wanted to make people laugh. It was something that just came to me naturally.

I downloaded Vine and made my first post on May 18, 2013. It took a while for me to figure out what to do with the app, but I knew that I wanted to do comedy. It was difficult for me to figure out what to do with six seconds. However, once I got the hang of it, my popularity grew quickly. I remember being excited that I had three followers. Then I remember being excited that I had 62. By the end of June, I had 80,000. By July, I had 400,000. After being on Vine for just four months, I had one million followers.

One of my first vines that became very popular was one in which I talked about girls saying "Haters be my motivators" so confidently only to turn around and question why people talk badly about them. It was a funny vine, and I think many people related to it. We all like to act like things people say about us don't bother us, but truthfully, they can hurt. It's unfortunate that people are often negative and we don't feel as though we have given them a reason to be that way.

So many good things have happened to me because of Vine. I've worked with many companies, endorsing their products on the app. I have been presented with television opportunities. There are celebrities following my Vine account. One of the most exciting things for me is the fact that my childhood idol, Anjelah Johnson who played Bon Qui Qui on MadTv, is now my friend! How many people can say that the person they grew up loving on television since sixth grade is a friend of theirs? It's amazing. So many great things have happened for me because of Vine.

The best advice I can give to anyone on Vine is that if you have more supporters than non-supporters, don't give up what you are doing. People like to say that they have haters. Let me tell you, I have haters. I have 4.6 million followers. That leaves a lot of room for hate comments, but I have learned to focus on the good things. For every hate comment I get, there are thousands of positive ones. It's not fair to my supporters, to the people who love me, to focus on the mean things people say. Why not focus on the nice comments instead? That's what I try to do. There are more of those anyway.

Remember what is important and don't let other people pull you down into their unhappiness.

# @Rob Johnston

I have been a dreamer for as long as I can remember. My parents tell long-winded tales of my wild creativity as a child. For example, as a two year-old boy, I was not content with just watching Sesame Street, or even just imagining myself as a Muppet. One morning, while my mother was doing whatever mothers do when they leave mischievous children unattended for a few moments, I discovered a stash of permanent markers. According to my parents, I proceeded to dye every inch of my head a solid green, leaving no spot unmarked. Then, I applied a brown marker to my forehead, creating a unibrow to really sell the look I was going for. My mother apparently shrieked at the sight of my green skin, and I replied in a very gruff voice, "I'm Oscar the Grouch!" I refused to break character for over an hour.

I am still that person. Fortunately, the Vine app has given me an outlet to share the zany, over-the-top ideas that flood my mind daily. Before Vine, I hadn't yet found a community of creative people in which I felt accepted. The landscape of Vine changes weekly. Popular trends take over, and are soon replaced by other fads, but the support that I have found for my particular brand of creativity has weathered the changing climates. For that, I am incredibly grateful.

In my life, I have never felt as though I truly fit in. I was friends with almost every clique in high school and college, but I didn't totally belong to any particular one group. Through this simple video application, I have found a group of like-minded people who appreciate the art and creativity in things that others may see as simple or stupid. One example of this is Vine artist Meagan Cignoli. She has become a very close friend, and we met completely through Vine. She has brought so much joy to my life and has inspired me both personally and creatively. Our vine styles are very different, and we work in different industries, but we have collaborated and developed a friendship that I value very much. It's crazy to think that we might never have met if it were not for Vine.

Vine has definitely changed my life. It's changed the way I view things; everything is a potential vine now! I've had several dreams come to fruition because of my work on the app. Some of these things might seem trivial in comparison with other truly life-changing experiences you will surely read in this book. But, for me, they were a really big deal.

My first vine was posted on February 7, 2013. It was a sketch in which my girlfriend shouted from another room, "Did you feed the dog?" Preoccupied by playing the piano like a maniac, I replied, "I took care of it!" The punch line of the vine was a shot of a stuffed toy dog lying dead surrounded by chocolate wrappers. It was simple, but my warped sense of humor landed me at the top of the popular page with 123 "likes" in six hours, which is a total joke now, but back then, it was a big deal. The challenge of telling a six-second story combined with the positive feedback I received for my quirky comedy made me fall in love with the app.

My vines have evolved a bit over the last year, but they have stayed true to my original love, which is telling a story. I try to bring simple jokes with strong visual gags to the table. I typically make all the costumes, sets, and oversized props in my vines. It has become part of the fun of producing these crazy little videos. The downside is that I am running out of room in my home. I have built around 15 large foam costumes including a seven-foot taco, a Vine logo, and an eight-foot sun outfit among many other things. Why? Because I love dreaming up things that seem impossible. I love hearing, "There's no way you can do that!" These are the things that fuel my creativity.

There is so much personal satisfaction that comes from spending hours setting up a scene or making a costume or filling a bathtub with an ungodly amount of something and then releasing it to the public to enjoy, criticize, love, or hate. Sure, it is great to feel the validation of an idea through positive audience response (that aspect has created more than a few ego monsters on Vine, but I digress), but what I have valued most has been the community, relationships, and support from other creative Viners.

I've also had the opportunity to visit the Jim Henson studios in Hollywood. I got to do a few vines with some of the puppets - another dream come true. I've gotten to meet Dick Van Dyke, Andy Milonakis, and Will Sasso –all of whom I had admired long before Vine. If you had told me a year ago that I would produce more than 500 six-second comedy bits and that they would be viewed by thousands of people, including my heroes, I don't think I would have believed you. But, I guess that's another way that Vine has changed me. I'm an even bigger dreamer now.

## @Marissa Mayne

I started using Vine around the end of May 2013. Before that, I was active on social media like Facebook and Twitter. I've always been considered "weird". I used to make funny YouTube videos and put them up for my friends to see. Someone told me about Vine and said it would be perfect for me since I enjoy making people laugh.

When I downloaded it, I didn't know how to use it. I wondered, "What would people do with this? It's only six seconds." I played around with it a bit, mostly watching other people. It didn't take me that long to figure it out. One day, I did an imitation of Nicki Minaj. Before I knew it, my vine got about 1,000 likes, which was a lot at that time. Within six months, I hit one million followers.

A favorite vine subject for my followers is my grandmother. My mother and I live with her. She is an angry person. It really bothered me when we moved in with her, but I have learned to just accept her for who she is. Just like everything else, I cope with it by making fun of the situation and laughing.

I get a lot of positivity in my comments; but I also get a lot of negativity. It doesn't really bother me. Hate comes with the territory. I get more love than hate, so I try to focus on that. What I have found is that I don't even have to respond to the mean comments. Other people do that for me. It's nice to see people take up for me. It shows me that they like me and they like what I do.

I have made many friends on Vine. Interacting with people and becoming part of the community has made me a better person, and I really mean that. The app has made me want to be a nicer person because of all the mean things I see being said and done. I've also had many great things happen in my life because of Vine. I've traveled and worked with "Team BullyProof" (teambullyproof.com). I've been helping promote the campaign. We are working to stop bullying and promote social change. It's something that I feel very strongly about and I am very proud to be a part of it. My mom is very proud of me. My whole family is, and that makes me feel good. My best advice for anyone on Vine is to just be you. There are too many standards. Every vine is hit or miss. Not everyone will like everything. Don't try to fit into the norm. People will see through it and you will not be happy.

# @*The White Trash Network*

I have always been creative and have always loved to make people laugh. As a child, I loved to act out skits and record them with a video camera. In my early social media days, I spent my weekends doing live, streaming video shows on JustinTV.com. I performed as different characters in my shows and sometimes there would be almost 200 people watching. My success on JustinTV led to my creating a YouTube channel called "The White Trash Network".

A friend told me about Vine, saying she thought I would do well on it. I thought it sounded ridiculous, as I couldn't imagine what anyone would do with six seconds, but, I gave it a try. My first vines were really dumb. I couldn't seem to find my niche. Eventually, I figured it out and became more comfortable. My first successful vine was of me acting like a "Sascrotch". I was in the woods and had a wig in my underwear that made me appear to have an insane amount of pubic hair. My sister filmed it and I ran toward the camera. People really liked it and I felt encouraged.

People have been so good to me on Vine. Before I downloaded the app and got comfortable with it, I always felt as though I had to perform as a character in order for people to like me. It makes me emotional to think about that, because I never thought people would actually like me for who I am. Why did I spend all that time hiding? On Vine, I learned that I didn't always have to act like someone else. I realized that I didn't have to hide behind funny costumes and voices. I could be myself and interact with people. In the process, I have made so many friends. It's such an awesome community.

As for trolls and negativity, I am quick to say something back, but I choose to do so with humor. I have not blocked a single person on Vine, and I won't give them that satisfaction, because they don't affect my life in any way. There are too many good things about Vine for me to focus on the bad parts. I've made friends in many different places.

People use the term "Attention Whore" as a negative thing. Truthfully, we are all attention whores. We like recognition. We like feedback. I like to make people laugh and I like to know that people enjoy it. Vine is perfect for that. I *could* survive without Vine, but I'm glad I don't have to, because it sure does make me happy.

# @*That Fatass Actually*

Naked. Born naked. Living naked. Life was simple. Boring, I dare say, and quiet. I grew up in a small town and then moved to an even smaller one when I became an adult. I had so much downtime that I had to make it interesting. I learned to entertain myself, to reach out, to adapt, and to expand myself. I had begun singing in church at the age of 14, all of which I did for love and acceptance.

Singing was the way in which I chose to share myself with people. It didn't require me to change who I was to please them, but it wasn't truly me. Other than singing, laughter was all I had. I tailored my personality to impress others. I was freakishly tall and heavy. At ten years of age, I was 5'6" and 175 pounds. To head off the fat jokes, I made up my own. I was very proactive. It seemed to work for me. Life carried on, and I grew up.

One day, a coworker told me about Vine. She insisted that I download it because of how much of a jackass I acted like on Twitter. "Just another damn app," I thought, but I did download it. I began following the popular Viners. That was a mistake. Annoyed with continually seeing the same jokes and characters, I set out to find something more, something fresh. I looked around for a while and, frustrated, thought about deleting the app. I had only about 60 followers anyway.

I've been involved in raising awareness for Cystic Fibrosis since 2012. My friend, Chelsea, has a little girl with the disease. Her name is Jaycee, and she is three years old. She is a remarkable little girl. Then, I came across a Viner who had about 180 followers. She made me laugh daily. She taught me how to use Assistive Touch and other things to richen my content. I watched her popularity balloon overnight. This got me to thinking. Could I use Vine to raise awareness for Cystic Fibrosis? So I set out on a mission. I'm still working on that mission.

With Vine, I could reach out to more people, but I needed more followers to work on my mission of raising awareness. I wanted to get more people to participate in the cause. How could I do that? I changed my Vine name from something innocuous to "That Fatass Actually" and started vining the most hilarious things I could come up with, but I guess I'm not as funny as I thought I was, or maybe I needed more than six seconds to get my point across. I hit a roadblock. "Maybe I need to vine with someone else to be funny. Or maybe I need to vine naked,"

So I vined naked.

All I showed in that one vine was my naked ass in my mirror. It blew up, and I gained
800 followers overnight. That was all fine and dandy, but I needed to continue entertaining those people, otherwise, I humiliated myself for nothing. Also, my friends in real life began using my vines as blackmail, threatening to show other people who were not on the app. One of them even showed my boss one of my vines. That is a moment I will never live down. Once my boss saw me twerking to a Snoop Dog song on Vine, my future in that company died instantly, but I had to keep going. The fundraiser for Cystic Fibrosis is coming

up soon, and I haven't even plugged it yet because I've been trying to build my following.

I'm taking it one day at a time, pressing onward. I am jobless, anxiously waiting to find out my fate. This may be the death of me. My car is up for repossession. I was recently told that I am "too qualified" to clean French fries out of the back seats of rental cars. I don't know whether I will ever get my job back. If there has ever been a low point in my life, this is it. I'm losing sight of what truly matters.

Vine is my escape. I'm not on Vine to be famous, or to make money. I'm on Vine for comfort and laughter. Vine is not about fame or money. It's about being yourself in front of millions of others. It's about the relationships that you build. It's about broadcasting your feelings. It's about getting support when you are emotionally naked.

Naked. That's what I am to my audience. Over 1,500 people look at my Vine page daily. They see me in all forms of emotions. They've seen me struggle to get a laugh out of them. They've seen me scream in defeat. They've seen my slurred drunkenness. They've felt my pain. My Vine, like my life, is naked.

## @Bryce Smooth

I've always been a goofy person, and I take pride in my ability to make people laugh. I'm also a musician who enjoys performing for an audience. Before Vine, I never really had an outlet to be ridiculous and get away with it. Before I moved to Northwestern Ontario, I was in a semi-professional band that had a lot of radio airplay and a hefty touring schedule.

I needed a way to feel as though I was still relevant in the world. I started using Vine in the late spring of 2013 after I saw a bunch of "Best Vine" videos pop up on Facebook. I thought some of them were absolutely hilarious, and they sparked my interest in the app.

My vine style is comedy. I rarely take myself seriously. I initially started using Vine by making the corniest jokes I could think of. As my Vine addiction grew, I began to push the boundaries more. I found ways to playfully torture my girlfriend, friends, and family. As time went on, I began coming up with more clever ideas. A few popular Viners shared my vines on their pages through revining and as a result, I gained more followers.

The only thing I really get from Vine is the satisfaction of making people laugh. I'm a firm believer in not taking yourself too seriously. I wouldn't say that Vine has changed my life, but it has definitely given me an opportunity to be immature and to let my freak flag fly. I'm a 12-year-old trapped in a 24-year-old's body, and any of my followers could surely attest to that.

## @*Chico Bronson*

In early 2013, I had several decent jobs, was just about to complete my second Masters degree, and was pretty happy. Life finally felt like it was on the right track, but something significant was missing. I couldn't quite put my finger on it, but I felt a little lonely, and I lacked the motivation and creativity that I formerly had. Everything felt bland, tasteless, and grey.

On the recommendation from a tech blog, I downloaded Vine to check it out in March of 2013. I was not convinced that such an app would have long-lasting appeal, since the videos were only a measly six seconds long, however, the more I watched, the more intrigued I became. First, I enjoyed the artistic, comedic elements of the popular page (when it was still worth watching). Marlo Meekins, Will Sasso, Keelayjams, Adam Goldberg and WhoisMaxwell were my favorites. They were clever, funny, and at times, very avant-garde. Every night, I'd scroll through my feed, laugh and marvel as Vine was becoming a part of my bedtime routine.

Late one night, however, I discovered that there was another layer of this world that I wasn't aware of. People were hanging out through their phones! It was astonishing to find the virtual equivalent of a late night pub, sitting in the palm of my hand. Every night, a growing group of talented weirdos would interact using several spontaneous themes to play off and inspire each other's talent. From singing, to dancing, to comedy, they'd riff back and forth and feed off each other's creative energy. This was the muse for which I yearned!

It became an obsession. Every night, I'd stay up until four in the morning with these lunatics. They called themselves the "Late Night Party Patrol" and played, laughed, and built wonderful relationships. It was amazing to find out how much you can grow to love a person you've never met in real life. These people grew to be my very dear friends.

These people sparked my desire to create and to entertain. I had always wanted to practice comedy through video, but never had the time to invest in editing and filming. With Vine, six seconds was all I needed. Vining became an obsession. I used it as a comedic sketchpad, capturing and developing jokes off the top of my head. In turn, I earned a reputation of a Blitzkrieg-style Viner.

That, however, wasn't enough. A few years before Vine, I had hit rock bottom in my social life and in my career. I was miserable, unmotivated, terribly anxious, and self-loathing. I had to rebuild myself, and through that rebuilding, I acquired some philosophical understandings about life, love, and self-confidence that entirely altered my perceptions. At every social opportunity I was granted, I would speak about how to feel accomplished, how to manifest your own destiny, how a person is entirely in charge of their own direction if they choose to be. What a great tool Vine could be to this end!

I began to reach out to people who seemed in need with a hash tag I called "Future Affirmations." Through this hash tag, I encouraged Viners and friends to pick something important they wanted to change about themselves and to commit to manifesting that change. People started responding to me, and through the effort I helped people feel comfortable in their own skin, motivated them to quit jobs, move homes, and take initiative to change their life for the better. It was so invigorating to be a positive force in the world.

As the app grew in popularity, the landscape started to change to a more hostile environment. The "status quo" started creeping in, homogenizing the creative landscape with meme-like pandering to the booming teen audience. My favorite comics, like Carlin, Prior and Hicks, were all people who chose to be "The Jester." They allowed themselves to be conduits of common sense through humor. The Jester is such a powerful personality archetype, because he holds a mirror up at his audience and reminds them that life is pretty ridiculous and silly. He reminds people that everyone is a hypocrite at one point in time or another. With all the disingenuous pandering, I felt that I had to become The Jester and shine a light on the absurd with humor, just as my heroes had done earlier.

I became an anti-hero of sorts in my circle of friends, deliberately throwing myself into various frays using sound logic but simultaneously, a deliberately obnoxious character to bring notice to people's unnecessary behavior through hyperbole, much like comedian Stephen Colbert. Like Colbert, the behavior usually yields mixed results. Currently, I feel a little embattled, because it can be a chore being a "voice of reason" in the din of insecure self-aggrandizing that can occur in the ego soup that is Vine. This is particularly true when people assume I'm genuinely being arrogant. In reality, I'm just confidently playing a character to absurdity and using the opportunity of an audience to spread the word that you don't have to accept the world as it is, but instead mold it into how you wish it to be.

That being said, the practice of playing "The Jester" has reassured me in my own beliefs and encouraged me to be able to commit even more long-lasting changes in my life. Thanks to Vine, I now have a plethora of amazing and talented friends who love me for me. This is a venue through which I can help people enact change in their lives and a soapbox from which I can share my beliefs to anyone willing to listen, and for that I'm forever thankful.

## @Justin Terio

Before Vine, I was a struggling musician. I still am. I've had various ups and downs as a singer in a band; I have played music with some big acts, had a song on the radio, and have done some international touring. I moved to Las Vegas from Ohio to pursue a relationship with a new manager in hopes of supporting my new band, "Lovesick Radio". I'm still here, plugging away. I can't say that much has changed since Vine came along, but I'm trying to implement some of the things I've learned from other Viners who use the app as a tool to promote their outside projects.

I began to vine on a whim after seeing some of Adam Goldberg's posts. He was producing amazing work, and I found him so inspiring. At that time, the magic of Vine was that everyone had an even playing field as far as editing was concerned. I was constantly amazed at the emotional, thought provoking, trippy, and creative vines he made. I jumped at the opportunity to use this amazing digital canvas to express myself.

My first vines were directly inspired by Goldberg. I tried different, creative camera angles and edits to create thematic sequences. I hadn't even considered comedy until I watched vines by Will Sasso, Steve Agee, and Marlo Meekins. Watching them, I had an epiphany.

I realized that Vine was a place for the class clowns to be clowns outside of a classroom. There is nothing better than a supportive, artistic community from which you can draw fountains of inspiration. Comedy is my true passion. With that being said, every vine I make is what I feel inspired to do in that moment. If laughter is the best medicine, I'm hoping to squeeze out as much as I can while I'm still able. Vine is a form of therapy for me. In turn, I hope that if people don't laugh at my vines they at least feel something after watching them.

My son was on Vine long before I was. We used to watch vines together and laugh. One day while we were out having dinner, I told him, "Let me try this. I'm funny. I can do this Vine thing." I posted my first few vines and had what I considered to be a fair amount of success with them. I vined whatever I wanted, whenever I wanted. I don't have a particular style. I just do what comes naturally to me. It has worked for me. Something I am very proud of is the fact that I have never asked people on Vine for favors or revines. My followers are there because they like what I do.

I am a character of myself in my vines. That means I don't hide myself, but I don't show people my struggles, either. Instead, I choose to be funny and make light of situations. I have problems just like anyone else, but I don't share those problems with many people.

I'm very careful about what I post on Vine. I am married. I am the mother of two sons. I want my family to be proud of me. I want my children to be proud of their funny mom who is popular on Vine, not embarrassed about things I am putting out there for the world to see. My sons are good boys who get excellent grades in school and are loved by their teachers and peers. I'm not going to do something on Vine to ruin that for them. I can be funny, edgy, and respectful simultaneously.

I get many comments calling me old. I'm 36, and that is far from old. I just have to laugh at the kids who say that. I'm just sitting here chilling on Vine. I'm set in life. I have a wonderful family, I look damn good, I'm funny, I'm successful in life and on Vine, and I'm just sitting back having a good time while they are still trying to figure out what they want to be when they grow up. Let them have fun calling me old. If trying to tear me down makes their day better, they can have at it.

I don't think I'm better than anyone else on Vine. There are people who think they are a form of royalty because they have high follower counts. I don't believe in that way of thinking or living. I've always said, "If you are the smartest person in your group, you need to find another group." We are always learning and growing. Not one of us is any better than the next person, and follower counts in no way, shape, or form should be used to gauge a person's status in life, or any respect, really.

Vine has really made a difference in my life. I have so much fun, and I laugh every day. What I love about it the most is that I get to laugh with my family. We look at vines together and laugh until our sides hurt. I've made many friends on the app also. I love meeting new people and getting to know genuine, sincere people. I look forward to finding out what comes next inside the world of Vine.

# Four

## Special Needs

# *@mattblackstock*

*By Cheryl Blackstock, Matthew's mother*

Matt is an autistic adult. It's remarkable how much Vine has helped him with his language and social skills. It's another way for him to communicate with others. Vine frees and empowers him.

He uses social media a lot, but he also has a lot of friends in the real world. He has a lot of friends from high school and church with whom he keeps in contact. It used to be difficult for him to socialize, but Vine has helped him get out of his shell. That's why I think it's so wonderful.

Matt was one of the first autistic kids to be mainstreamed into an elementary school in Buncombe County, North Carolina. I began working with him when he was 16 months old. In school, he did great in math and reading, but he couldn't vocalize. We went to a speech therapist, and he began talking. He had to repeat the first grade, which was a hard, but necessary decision. In middle school, he received an award for the "most outstanding student". Everyone loved him. It was a proud moment for us both.

He received a certificate of completion from high school and has been working at a retirement home for almost eight years. He drives a moped to work. He enjoys the job and his coworkers so much that, when it snows, he will walk to work. His supervisors and coworkers greatly appreciate him, and he recently got a raise.

Matt has always been sensitive about the way he talks. Recently, someone on Vine asked him what was wrong with his voice. That person even went so far as to accuse Matt of faking his way of speaking. Matt had become so proud of the progress he was making with coherent speech, and then that happened. There was a tremendous amount of support from the Vine community. It was wonderful to see the camaraderie from so many Viners who stepped forward and spoke up for him. People made vines to help cheer him up and let him know he was valued and loved.

Matt is interested in technology. He enjoys music and plays guitar. People can tell he is special, but Matt possesses many gifts. He knows he has autism, and he is willing to talk about it. If you have a sincere question for him, don't be afraid to ask. It's good for him to answer them.

I think most people are good-hearted. I see that a lot of that on Vine, and I appreciate it.

# @*Joshua & Ethan*

Ethan has Angelman Syndrome, a medical condition similar to autism. Our first few vines were just the two of us hanging out, riding bikes and doing other silly things. One day, we found Tobie Stevens on Vine. At that point, she had about 7,000 followers. Ethan adored her, and he would scroll through all her vines, watching them over and over. I decided to help him make a vine saying, "Tobie, I love you! I love you!" When she saw it, she revined it. That day, we started a great friendship with her that we know we will have for life.

We gained many followers when she revined us, so I decided to make more videos. People say that they enjoy our posts and that our vines make them happy. They make Ethan happy too. We want to share the love that we are shown on Vine. Our lives have changed from all the wonderful comments. We make vines because we love making positive changes in people's lives.

Ethan has always had a smile on his face, even during his surgical and recovery periods. His inner happiness has continually shined through. As a paramedic, I strive to help people in real life as well as on Vine; an app that I mistakenly thought was a game about trees when I first heard about it. As long as there are people out watching our vines, we will try to make their days better.

## *Annie and Sean*

I started vining in the summer of 2013, just to make family videos. In I stumbled upon @Vine Comfort Team (VCT), an account in which people were bravely sharing their struggles. I decided to make a vine not only to share my love for my child Sean, but also to share my fear that he had autism. Sean was one and a half years old at the time. I had seen many signs of autism in him, but I was unsure whether he had it. I was terrified at the thought of finding out that he did.

After sharing our struggles with VCT, I received an outpouring of love and support from hundreds of people I didn't know. Many of those people were parents of children with autism. I instantly had a community of supporters that I could call on for advice and support.

I gained the courage to not be ashamed or wallow in self-pity. Through the power of the friendship and support that I had gained on Vine, I felt ready to tackle my fears. Almost immediately after sharing my situation on Vine, I had Sean evaluated, and I enrolled him in developmental, occupational, and speech therapies.

During the next few months, I vined everything. I filmed all his therapy sessions, learning sign language, our joys, our struggles, his birthday, diet changes, and random pieces of our everyday life. As more people began to follow our journey, we began to share even more. The love and support from our Vine friends kept us going strong.

In February 2014, Sean was officially diagnosed with autism. Although it was a sad day, we were surrounded with the love and support of our Vine friends. Like any other parent and child, we have good days and bad, however, I am so thankful that Vine has allowed us to document these intimate moments of our life. It has been immensely helpful and cathartic to share our journey.

I believe that our vines have helped other parents who found themselves in similar situations. It is my hope that we are creating more autism awareness through our sharing. Most of all, I hope that we are showing a normal, loving family with a very awesome little boy named Sean, who just happens to have autism.

## *Yolanda Baker*

When my son, Luke, was diagnosed with autism at age eighteen months, my husband, Mark, and I did everything we could to get him the best therapy for his condition. By the end of the first twelve months, we had spent thousands of dollars on treatments that were not covered by insurance. We suffered both financially and emotionally. We had no idea what Luke's future would be.

It has been six years since his initial diagnosis. I am grateful for the tremendous help we have received from medical professionals, teachers, and family members. I'm confident that no matter what happens to Luke, Mark and I will raise him to be the best autistic person he can be in a neurotypical world.

There are rare times where I feel like a fish, wanting to lay low at the bottom of a placid stream, however, most of the time I feel like ramming head-on with anything that gets in the way of becoming the best person I can be. Vine is an outlet that allows me to express myself. The app gives me that little push I need, usually as a laugh to get me through my next phone call or doctor's appointment.

I can't say that Vine has changed my life, but it has definitely helped me deal with daily stresses in ways that no other social media app has. Facebook, LinkedIn, Twitter, and other online tools are great, and they have helped me expand my consulting work along with aiding me in writing two books, but there is something about the immediacy and instant gratification of Vine that kick starts my day and inspires me to keep pressing forward.

*Five*

*Artists*

# @Tony Oswald aka @Tony Besides

Interview with Tony Oswald by Jen Dent

*Tony Oswald grew up in Glasgow, Kentucky. He studied Broadcasting at Western Kentucky University and moved to New York City for an internship. He has lived there ever since. He is now a film and television editor and is married to Katie (aka @Katie Besides), a schoolteacher.*

*Oswald has received much attention for his Vine series: @Tony Besides, a "comic's tragedy" centered on adultery and the divorce of a young marriage told through 725 six-second Vine posts. Tony wrote and directed the human narrative drama, (the first and only of its kind on Vine), with the help of @Megan Burke (aka @Alana Burkeside). Tony, Katie, and Burke are the main characters of the series.*

*The series wrapped on March 19, 2014 to raving reviews from Viners.*

**JD: When did you first get on Vine?**

TO: March 14, 2014.

**JD: What was your life like before Vine? Did you use social media?**

TO: Oh, yes. I was pretty much addicted to Facebook, but, I didn't use Facebook like most people use it, announcing my daily activities or what I was eating. I used Facebook for comedy. I enjoyed putting jokes and observations out there and seeing what kind of feedback I got. It became a sort of obsession, because I eagerly awaited the responses I would receive.

I was known in my circle of friends as being "the funny guy" on Facebook. I would meet people that I didn't really know, and they would tell me how much they enjoyed following me on there. I would often get embarrassed recalling things I had said or done. In the end, I have always had the philosophy that I would not guard myself too much on social media. What you see is what you get and generally, it has worked quite well for me.

**JD: Did you do any type of videos on social media prior to Vine?**

TO: Not really. I did a YouTube animation once that went viral. It was pretty strange, actually. It got about 750,000 views. I didn't really take the time to do any more of them.

Prior to that, I was a film student, so I've always been involved in that type of media. Before Vine, I had just finished editing a feature ("Frames" available on Vimeo). Other than the YouTube animation and things I was doing for work, I wasn't doing any types of videos for social media feedback.

**JD: What were your early vines like?**

TO: I was doing comedy. That was my thing, just like with Facebook. People seemed to like it.

**JD: How did your style change?**

TO: I wouldn't really say that my style changed, however, there is a very big part of me, as you can see with the Besides series that is very introspective, expressive, and not comedic at all. I love being funny, but there is more to my life than comedy. I found that whenever I posted vines that were not particularly funny, people did not like them.

**JD: Why do you think that is?**

TO: I'm not really sure. I think people just get used to you doing one thing, one style, and if you change up on them, they don't quite know what to think of it. People tend to want to box you in.

**JD: So, tell me why you created @Tony Besides.**

TO: I felt the need to be creative in other ways. I created the Besides account to be able to post what I wanted, when I wanted, as much as I wanted. I wanted to post on a whim without thinking too hard about it. Very early on, I began to use the third-person narrative.

**JD: I remember seeing it and thinking how creative and original it was. Soon after that, however, many people started doing their own Besides accounts. What are your thoughts on that?**

TO: I have to be very selective in how I answer that. First, I was flattered and humbled. I continue to feel that way to this very day. I was ecstatic at the positive feedback I was receiving, and I felt that if people were inspired to be creative and make vines in that voice it was a good thing. I don't think most of the Besides accounts are accurate depictions of what I started with the idea, but that's okay. Everyone is different, and if people enjoy it and get something positive out of it that is all that matters.

**JD: You have had mostly positive feedback, but I noticed that some people did not like the Besides at all. Some people seemed to take offense to it. Why is that?**

TO: I'm not exactly sure. People have interpreted it how they want. All I'm doing is telling a story and everyone will take it differently. Some people will like it. Some people won't. Some people will become invested in the story further. Some people will get angry. It's just like any other movie or television show. You aren't really doing a good job with storytelling if you don't elicit a vast array of emotions in your viewers.

**JD: I've noticed that you have been called "pretentious" a lot. Why do you think that is?**

TO: That seems to be the number one insult. Again, I'm not quite sure. Vine is a place known originally, for goofy comedy. I chose to do this human narrative drama in the third person, and I took it very seriously. That bothered people, but people are bothered every day by television shows, movies, and songs. It just happens.

*Note: In early January 2014, the @Tony Besides story took a shocking turn. This vine was entitled "The Art Hung Crooked on the Wall" and depicted nudity and simulated sex. This will forever go down in Vine history as one of the most talked-about posts.*

**JD: "The Art Hung Crooked on the Wall."**

TO: *Laughter*

**JD: Let's talk about that, shall we?**

TO: *More laughter*

**JD: What did you think would happen once people saw that?**

TO: I knew people would flip out. I thought I would lose at least 1,000 followers. What I didn't know was that it would turn into at least a 24-hour meme. I was shocked at all the remakes, parodies, comments, and even the criticisms.

**JD: Everyone wants to know what your wife, Katie, thought of that.**

TO: We discussed it at length before deciding to go through with it. We told our close friends and family what would happen so that no one would see it, and become upset. We are a real-life married couple, and like every other couple in the world, we have our problems. We didn't want people who cared about us to think that this was actually happening outside of the story.

**JD: Some viewers got really upset.**

TO: They did. I think the reason is that they know this type of thing happens very frequently. I think it hit home for many people, whether it sparked jealousy, fear, or memories of bad times in their relationships. Again, each person is different, and people will interpret and react in their own ways.

**JD: I thought it was amazing. I'm sad to see that it is over, but I understand that the story has reached its end. What are your plans now?**

TO: I'm working on turning the Besides series into a feature-length film. I think I've reached the end of my time with Vine. I'm not sure. This is the most exciting; fulfilling thing I have done to date. I'm very proud of it, and I appreciate all the support I have received.

I'm not certain what comes next for me as far as Vine is concerned, but I have to say that I am really grateful that I discovered it. It has opened so many doors for me.

## @R E Medlin

Before Vine, I was a normal person who woke up every day, ate breakfast, went to work, drove home, played with my son, and sometimes got to watch a film. My life was like a loop that went on forever. Vine, with its own six-second, looping videos, changed that. Prior to Vine, I hardly ever used my phone. I now use my phone like every other insane person on this planet and I blame Vine for that. It is an infuriatingly addictive app, causing me to both love and hate Vine.

My brother, Jason, first introduced me to Vine during the first week of June, 2013. He had been exploring it for a few months and talked in great detail about the immense creativity on it. He insisted that I download it. I was extremely reluctant, and I didn't understand why anyone would want to make something only six seconds long much less watch or enjoy it. He urged me to explore it for at least a week. After only a few hours of watching @Vi and Vie, @j_e__s___s, and @Adam Goldberg, I was astonished beyond words at what I was seeing.

For the first two weeks, I engulfed myself in the beautiful creations being posted. What intrigued me the most was the diversity of expression. There is a corner for everyone on Vine. Animation, stop-motion sunsets, comedy, drama, avant-garde, exploration, and moments of everyday life from everyday people all over the planet, all making up just a fraction of what can be found on the app. I continued watching as many vines as I could in my free time, and I became inspired to try my own. I wanted to get accustomed to how the filming worked, so I helped some friends make vines on their accounts. As for myself, I experimented with basic techniques like stop-motion sunsets and simple montages, but I did not post anything on my own account

There were rumors that Instagram would add a video option. I honestly held off posting anything on Vine because of the popularity of Instagram. I had the intention of going to Instagram to create my videos; however, I broke down and created my first vine on June 19, 2013. It involved artificial rain from a hose and two six-year-old kids. After nine ridiculous takes and two wet, grumpy children, I gave up and went with what I had.

The very next day, Instagram was updated to include video. I deleted Vine from my phone, assuming everyone would flock to Instagram and make beautiful content such as I had been enjoying on Vine. I waited, but nothing happened. I watched some videos, but the quality were poor, and the entertainment value was minimal if not obsolete. Most importantly, the content did not loop, it just abruptly ended.

After seeing this, I knew that Vine was clearly the place for what I planned on creating. Not only that, but Viners were continuing to make content that blew my mind, made me laugh, or made me just appreciate being alive. All these things were still happening in just six seconds. Eleven days after leaving Vine, I re-downloaded the app and made my second post. I will remain on Vine as long as it exists.

I post very infrequently due to a lack of time, and obsessive perfectionism, (yet another reason for my love/hate relationship with the app), yet I am experimenting every time I make a vine. I am not sure how to label my style. Most of my ideas come from still photos I want to see come to life or from the cinema. I approach all of my ideas with character back stories so that I can make something as close to a piece of narrative storytelling as possible.

People have told me that my vines are dark, but I have trouble seeing that point of view. Some of my content does deal with death or torture, but I see that as experimentation on people's reactions. My vines are also often labeled as pretentious. I really just want to make something that will make people feel some sort of emotion. I am making something that I love, hate, fear, or will laugh about.

Everybody loves to be expressive. With Vine, there are endless opportunities. Sometimes I hold onto my vines in my drafts for a few days because I don't want to give them away. I want to keep them for myself for as long as I can. I feel that once they are posted, they are no longer mine; they belong to everyone else. The viewers mold it into something more than what I intended it to be. I really don't get much out of making vines; rather, I get more out of my love for the Vine community. I have met so many incredible people who have shared their lives, art, and creativity.

I have met friends who inspire me to be creative, happy, and to love the world I am in. I never imagined that an app on a phone could be this powerful. It clearly is the most powerful app ever developed. I am curious to see where it goes.

# @Jess Matsumoto

*Piece written by Jen Dent based on conversations with Jess Matsumoto.*

Jess Matsumoto, a woman of few words, intrigues me. Her work on Vine is amazing, so much so that she is verified with relatively few followers compared to most people who have received verification on the app. When I initially asked her to submit a piece for this book, she sent three sentences, which only intrigued me more. I decided to use those three sentences and place them on a still photograph from what I consider to be one of her most amazing Vines: "RIP John Lennon—Number Twenty-Four in the Dead Musician Series". This was a vine that she created with the help of @Ameera Belle.

"I will always be greatful to the Vine Platform for what it gave me, and what it continues to give many people. It gave me a new job, new friends, and a new life. Thank you to the Vine creators and programmers."
- Jess Matsumoto

After receiving this short statement from Jess, I contacted her and asked if we could talk on the phone. I felt strongly about including her in this book because let's face it; I'm in awe when I watch her work on Vine. After talking with her, these are the things I learned.

She grew up on the east coast before moving to Los Angeles to pursue acting. While there, she lived the life of a struggling actress, often moving from place to place and sometimes sleeping on couches in friends' homes. She worked hard auditioning and was a member of an improv group while in LA.

She says that she discovered Vine and used it as a "sketch pad," of sorts, posting vines with subjects that ranged from comedy, blog-like material, and introspective themes. Some of her most memorable work was the #DeadMusicians Series in which she used elaborate sets and costumes to portray deceased artists such as Amy Winehouse, John Denver, Lou Reed, and Mama Cass, to name a few.

Jess says that the Dead Musician Series was actually an attempt to win the heart of a man she was interested in, and it worked. Not only did Vine help her do that, but it also earned her a highly sought-after position in an advertising company in Washington, DC. The company had seen her vines, and after becoming so impressed with her creativity and artistic abilities, hired her out of many applicants who may otherwise have been considered to be more qualified for the position. Because of Vine, she has a stable, fulfilling career in a field that makes her happy and is currently in a great relationship.

Recently, on Vine, a person commented, "If Vine has changed your life, that's pretty gay." Matsumoto replied, "If getting a position at an ad agency and making profound relationships is 'gay', then I'm a flaming homosexual."

## @Mike Bennett

I live in a small college town in Central Pennsylvania. I have been doing a podcast for two years now (www.popularoutcasts.com) with two friends. My friends and I have been very successful with our podcast, and we are popular with the college crowd. I like to think that we have been instrumental in changing the way the locals think about certain important topics. I have also been running an open mic comedy show since September 2013.

I heard about Vine from one of my podcast partners. I downloaded it in July, 2013, but I didn't start vining until around September. I was very active on Twitter and Facebook, almost to the point of addiction. Vine changed all that. I hardly get on either of those sites anymore.

I was working at an art gallery and had a lot of free time on my hands. At first, I spent a lot of time watching vines. I knew that I could do something great with Vine, but I couldn't figure out how to use the six-second time frame in a way that would be entertaining to anyone. When I decided to make some of my own, they were your typical first vines like anyone else did. I vined my cat. I made some bad stop motion videos. I tried to do some sketch comedy, but quickly realized that wasn't my niche. I've deleted all those vines since then.

The first vine I had success with was one in which I drew Super Mario from the video games, and I posted it on the art channel on Vine. I'm not even sure how people found me, but they did. I do know that the revine button is responsible for getting me the exposure I received. My content is family-friendly, so I didn't think I would get that much attention, but I had a few lucky strikes in the form of Viners with bigger numbers revining me. Because of that, more people saw my content.

As an artist, it means the world to have my creations seen by other people. Vine has done that for me; it's a portfolio. I've done quite a bit of commissioned work for people who have asked me to draw things for them. Also, I've had some unimaginable opportunities open up for me that I only dreamed of before Vine. It's amazing what has happened for me simply because I downloaded this little phone app.

Vine has greatly improved my self-esteem as far as my work is concerned. I'm a very humble person, and I tend to downplay my artistic abilities. What I have found is that I am no longer able to ignore my own talents. When you have over 20,000 watching you and telling you that you're doing a great job, you eventually have to give in and acknowledge yourself. It hasn't been easy; we are all our own worst critics, but Vine has helped me in that aspect of my life immensely.

My advice to Viners is this: Vine is about the community. Yes, your content matters, but you have to be social to get the full experience that Vine has to offer. If you are not interacting with your followers and other Viners, you are not getting the full experience of the app. I get on to find out what other people are doing and to support them. Good things have come to me because of that.

## @Le Seb Ettinger

I've always had some sort of creative outlet. I spent my college years being a DJ at raves and clubs. After I stopped doing that, I missed the act of selecting and mixing records. I've always been very music-oriented, and I have a vast collection of vinyl and digital records that span many genres. Photography has long been a passion of mine as well; it happens to be what I studied in college and what I now do for a living.

I downloaded the Vine app in the spring of 2013. At first, I didn't know what to make of it, so I just played around. I really enjoyed the looping aspect of Vine and so I mostly made video mashups, combining music and lyrics with YouTube videos. Most of my vines were silly and comical with the occasional serious subject being thrown into the mix.

The "Vintage Floridamericana" style that I'm most known for is the result of a car accident (which, for the record, was not my fault). After the accident, I was driving a rental car that had XM satellite radio. I've always loved jazz, swing, blues, and rock n roll. I found myself listening to the 40's and 50's stations. Listening to those stations, I became interested in the hopeful, yet melancholy sounds of that era juxtaposed with the decaying South Florida landscape, shrouded in tropical flora and populated with interesting characters. I loved the random and unforgiving nature of vining while I drove and listened, using live radio (no choice of song, no rewinding, no second takes) while shooting whatever I happened to drive past.

Visually, I tend to approach my vines as I approach my photography. I try to make simple, yet interesting compositions of mundane subjects or landscapes. Creating seamless audio loops is also important to me. I definitely suffer from "loop OCD" and delete many posts that I'm unhappy with. As for why I do it, I don't really know. Since I was young, I've always been driven to create things. Vine allows me to do so quickly, easily, anywhere, anytime, and then immediately share it with others.

Vine offers me a tremendous amount of creative satisfaction, but equally importantly, I derive much inspiration and entertainment from so many artists who I have discovered through the app. Some of the inspiration has directly influenced my work, but mostly I love seeing people's development and growth as artists.

Vine has reawakened my need to discover new forms of expression. It has given me more confidence in my own creative abilities. Vine has provided me with a simple, yet powerful platform to explore and combine different passions. Most importantly, it has introduced me to a creative community to share with and be inspired by. I want to thank the Vine team for creating such a revolutionary platform. As I'm sure this book will reveal, it has had a positive impact on many people's lives. I want to also thank those who create positive, original content, as well as the people who support and encourage them.

# @DeathSmoKe

I have always been creative. I spent much of my childhood alone with my imagination as a best friend. My imagination is so good, that I felt like I was a professional musician before I even played an actual instrument! I used to make elaborate Lego creations, and would add every toy I owned into a stage show. Star Wars, He-Man, and Thundercats were all family members in my bizarre daily circus that I put on for my eyes only.

As an adult, I have saturated my life in music and film. I challenge myself to always be artistic. I continually experiment with all forms of artistic media including music, painting, poetry, photography, and film. The videos I made when I was younger were much like the vines I make today. They are composed of short clips of bizarre images mixed with light and dark humor. They were all made for my own enjoyment, although I have shared some of them with close friends throughout the years. I never quite understood what I was supposed to do with my art other than to enjoy it myself. I uploaded some of my videos to YouTube, but I didn't have any idea how to build an audience.

All that changed the instant I discovered the Vine app on April 7, 2013. I was immediately enthralled by the idea of a six-second video. I didn't even watch a single vine before I made my first post. I have always strayed from distractions that may influence the ideas that I already have in my mind. For example, when I'm trying to write music, I refrain from listening to any music at all. I don't want to be pushed in any direction by outside forces. Vine changed that as well.

As I sorted through countless vines, I found the vast variety to be unbelievably refreshing. I discovered blooming stars around every corner. In the beginning, I wasn't very impressed by most of the humor I saw. Jokes get old very quickly. I was more interested in seeing life being lived in places I had never been before. It was amazing to find people who were vining their daily activities. I felt as though I were actually a part of their lives. I went on dates with their girlfriends, to museums around the world, and even traveled down The Seine.

Vine is solely responsible for my "creative rebirth". Before Vine, my life went through some monumental changes. I had been through a horrible divorce after discovering that my wife was having an affair with my best friend, who also happened to be my boss. Naturally, I didn't keep that job. They lied to me about their betrayal for two years until I discovered it through a series of texts between them. Talk about a mind fuck. A broken heart is easy to heal compared to a broken mind and shattered spirit.

Not long afterwards, a new woman entered my life. She was not connected in any way to my circle of longstanding friends, so it was easy to drop out of sight and shelter myself from almost everyone I knew. I became somewhat of a hermit, and I didn't mind. I was happy and in love. On March 14, 2013, however, (which also happened to be my birthday), I received a heartbreaking text from my girlfriend. It was heartbreaking because she meant to send it to the man with whom she was cheating on me. Go figure.

I hadn't used any form of social media since MySpace was at the height of its popularity. I tried Facebook, but the moment I finalized my account and reached the "find friends" stage, the first person Facebook suggested to me was my ex-wife. The next person it suggested was the guy she cheated with. It was like some sick joke was being played on me. I wanted nothing to do with it after that. I needed to find an outlet for my creativity.

When I began vining, I was happy to have found an outlet for my creativity. Not only did I find an audience, I discovered some of the finest talent and the greatest people I've ever known. I have found genuine human beings that share the same views as I. They are caring, supportive people who I feel as though I have known for a lifetime. I developed instant connections to people unlike I'd ever had before. I never would have believed that something like this could happen. The only people who completely understand this feeling are the people on Vine.

My vines are always experimental. I'm a self-taught artist in almost every aspect. If I have an idea, I usually do it immediately. I test the waters and I post it, whether it's perfect or not. I make vines of everything and anything I can think of, while being inspired by others. I am inspired by their vines, but more so by their support and encouraging words. They make me want to share the way I see the world. That is a piece of me that most people never notice or understand.

# @j_e__s___s

Note from Jen Dent:

I wanted to include @j_e__s___s in this book because she is another one of my favorite Viners. I found her Vine account on a Saturday night and spent at least two hours going through every single one of her posts. Every time I watched a new one, I swore it was my favorite. I was mesmerized and floored by what I was seeing. I sat with my mouth gaping open at what she was doing in her vines. I left a comment telling her that she was an "amazing freak".

I had never seen such creativity in my life. She was taking six seconds of time and posting vines that were beautiful, heart breaking, shocking, horrific, and hilarious. One moment, she was pretending to try to play a song on a recorder with fake teeth in, only to be interrupted by her cat, Jack. The next moment, she was creating a lifelike painting of that same cat on a canvas with blood from a scratch he had given her. I couldn't stop watching.

Like Jess Matsumoto, j_e__s___s is a woman of few words. She does not give herself nearly enough credit in this piece; as a matter of *fact, she doesn't talk about her gifts at all. I could NOT write this book without including her in it. She's amazing.*

Honestly, it is difficult to remember my life before Vine. I was employed (and still am), and spent most of my free time taking care of a handicapped parent. Any moment I had between the two was wasted. Creatively, I felt as though I was at a standstill. My job was in a monotonous production phase and offered very few opportunities to exercise my mind.

One day, my buddy, Chris, told me that I should download this "Vine thing" because people were posting all kinds of stuff and it was interesting to watch. I downloaded the app, and I did a few boring vines of my cat, Jack, just to give it a try. Within the next week, I found myself opening up to it more and more. I felt as though I had discovered a whole other world inside Vine. There were real people posting real things, and I had a front row seat.

I can't pinpoint when Vine went from a people-watching, time-killing opportunity to a creative outlet for me, but soon my head was spinning with ideas. For a while, I posted whatever I found interesting without realizing people were taking notice. Strangers were complimenting me on silly little things I posted, and that is what fueled the fire. I began interacting with people who commented on my vines and, since then, the app has been nothing short of an insane, social, creative phenomenon in my life.

I've made real friends that I talk to every day, several whom I have met in real life. I've traveled to places to meet people. I have people with whom I can bounce ideas off and vice versa, and sometimes we collaborate on projects. Vine has given me a creative outlet and introduced me to people who genuinely make my life better. None of this would have happened had I not downloaded this app.

I'm not sure where Vine will end up. As for me, it is something that sparked my creative enthusiasm again, and for that, I am incredibly grateful.

Before Vine, I was not terribly different from myself now. I was happy, and I felt accomplished. I had a beautiful wife and daughter and lived in a charming, modest house in a great neighborhood. I had built up a successful insurance and risk management business and achieved the status of being considered an expert in my field. I was an avid surfer, skier, runner, and had recently completed an Ironman distance triathlon. Life was good, but there was definitely something lacking.

Growing up, I always had some sort of creative outlet, and I enjoyed entertaining. I spent a lot of time writing and drawing when I was a kid. In college, I took some film courses, but I never felt as though I had the time or equipment to make a decent film. I worked as an emcee at a comedy club and had built up a 20-minute set, but I never took it seriously because I wasn't interested in the life of a stand-up comedian. I chose my career with the idea that I would be able to make time for creative pursuits, but I soon found out that when you work for yourself, you tend to work more than you don't. For about eight years, I did almost nothing creative at all.

I began using Vine on March 29, 2013. I intended to use it simply to share short videos of my daughter with family and friends, much in the way I use Facebook and Instagram. My first few vines are of my daughter crawling around. It didn't take long for me to start telling little stories and making jokes.

I began to realize that people liked what I was doing on Vine. Around a month after I started using it, I noticed that one of my vines had over 700 "likes" on it. I didn't think it was a particularly good vine; in fact, I would probably say that it was awful. It did, however, plant a seed. People often say that you shouldn't care about "likes," but I can't say that it's not enjoyable when I receive instant, positive feedback on something that I created. I think the important thing is to not become a slave to the "likes" or opinions of others and to be true to yourself.

As far as art is concerned, I honestly didn't even try to vine anything that I considered artistic until I saw that I had an audience that liked what I was doing. Even now, I try to remember the reason I started Vining whenever I feel like I'm taking it too seriously. I like to keep in mind that the only reason I originally developed an audience at all is because I have an extraordinarily cute daughter who happens to be my biggest inspiration.

It's not easy to describe what I do other than to simply say it's "very me." Outside my shooting style and my tendency to mix short cuts with images that I find compelling, I don't think I really even have a "vine style." I like to tell stories, but I get bored quickly when I try to stick to a specific theme. I know that this has probably worked against me in the popularity game, but that's okay with me. Repetition bores me. I like to keep things fresh. That being said, there are definitely a few recurring themes in my vines: Film Noir, existentialism, confused identity, false memory/history, and a touch of anti-authoritarianism. I also like to use humor, mainly in the form of sarcasm, whenever I can.

In the first few months, Vine was a huge confidence booster. I knew that I could entertain people from my comedy club days, but I didn't think too much of it. In addition, I have spent some great moments with my daughter as I document her growing up. I can't wait to show them to her when she's old enough to appreciate them. I've been paid to make a vine, and I have a couple more paid opportunities coming up, but that's just a bonus for me. Finally, I have made some fantastic friends, some of whom I've had the pleasure to meet in person.

Vine has renewed my interest in film and inspired me to explore my creativity. I've started to work on a few films outside of Vine. Without the app, I would never have done this. I'm not sure that film will become anything more than a hobby for me, but I now realize that there is that potential. The best, unintended result of Vine has definitely been the friendships I have made. I have become part of a fantastic community.

## *@Corduroy Cat aka @Frankie Cordero*

I've been interested in puppetry since I was very young. Like most kids, I loved The Muppets and Sesame Street. From the age of three years old I wanted to know more about what went on behind the scenes of those shows. My parents would take me to live puppet shows around Chicago. I was entertained by the stories but also wanted to know how the puppets worked. Even at that young age, I recognized that there was a lot of work involved in putting on a performance like that.

At the age of eight, I began building my own puppets. While I was learning to do this, my dad took me to the library to check out some books on the subject. A librarian told me about the Chicagoland Puppetry Guild. That year, I attended my first Puppeteers of America Festival. When I was ten years old, I began performing with my puppets for birthday parties, libraries, festivals and other live events. I continued to do so through my high school years.

I applied to the Puppetry program at the University of Connecticut during my junior year of high school. During high school, I had met David Rudman, a puppeteer with his own puppet company in Illinois. He also worked on Sesame Street. David gave my audition tape to Kevin Clash, then a puppet coordinator on the show. I began working with them occasionally during my freshman year in college, taking bus trips from Storrs, Connecticut to New York City. This opened many doors for me. Currently, I'm working in productions such as the New York Metropolitan Opera, "Madama Butterfly" and most recently, "Walking With Dinosaurs," which is on a national tour featuring life-sized animatronic dinosaurs. I've had the pleasure of working as a puppeteer/director for various TV shows, commercials and music videos for clients such as PBS, Nickelodeon, Noggin, MTV, and Comedy Central.

I built the Corduroy Cat puppet for a music video, "Hello Again," for The Gregory Brothers. The video features a couple of stuffed animals that come to life. My musician and puppeteer friends and I made a few more YouTube music videos using the puppet. I wasn't very active on social media. I had Facebook and Twitter accounts, but I didn't use them that often. Vine changed all of that.

In August 2013, a friend told me about Vine. It sounded interesting to me, and I had been looking for a way to share my content, but I wasn't sure how to go about doing it. I wanted to produce more work and share it with people. YouTube was a way to do that, but there was no sense of community and producing music videos meant needing to gather a crew of people together for each shoot. I wanted to be able to shoot on a small camera by myself. The Vine app features also took me back to my roots of in-camera editing, practical effects and stop-motion- all techniques I used as a kid, shooting puppet videos on my father's bulky VHS camcorder. I've found a wonderfully creative community on Vine where I can share my love for puppetry, and interact with other creative people.

# Six

## Mental Health

Growing up, I suffered from social anxiety and awkwardness. I was overweight during most of my high school years, and I was continuously picked on. I didn't talk to, or hang out with anyone. I didn't do anything unless it was with my family, I was so self-conscious. If I was in public and I heard someone laughing, I would immediately assume they were laughing at me.

I never tried to make friends because I was afraid of being picked on even more than I already was. I remember asking myself, "Why would anyone want to hang out with me?" I was miserable. I heard a little voice in my head telling me that until I realized just how much I wanted to change, I wouldn't be able to motivate myself enough to do something about it. During the summer before my senior year, I went on vacation for a week. When I got back home, I finally realized just how tired I was of being miserable and unhappy with myself every day. I decided to lose weight. Not quite two years later, I'm eighty-five pounds lighter and multiple clothing sizes smaller.

My sister, Kelsey, is the one who introduced me to Vine. First, I thought it was pointless, but I decided to give it a chance and as I did, I actually grew to love it. For the longest time, I only revined things. I used Vine to get a good laugh when I needed it. Who doesn't need a good laugh now and then?

Although I had lost a lot of weight and was happy about it, I still suffered from social anxiety. I wanted to make my own vines, but I feared being picked on again. Most of all, I feared failure because I had gotten used to succeeding. I knew that it would be out of my comfort zone to vine myself. I was afraid, but I learned that not everyone will like you.

Vine is far from being pointless. It isn't "just an app." It's so much greater than that. I find it to be almost impossible to describe. I consider my Vine friends as part of my family. Although we may never actually meet the friends we have met through Vine in real life, they are right there in my pocket. Vine has made such a positive impact on so many peoples' lives from all over the world. My life is the complete opposite from what it was before. I'm so happy with myself.

I love my life and the people who are in it, both in my real life and on Vine. I would not change a thing. It feels great. I can't say that I no longer have social anxiety, I still do, but I can say that it doesn't even come close to affecting me now as much as it used to. If I haven't learned anything else over this amazing journey, I did learn one thing. I learned that until we can love ourselves, it's absolutely ridiculous to expect someone else to love you.

## @Janine Hogan

I'll never forget the first time I had a Grand Mal seizure. I was nine years old and had fallen asleep on my mom's bed the night before. I somehow ended up on the floor. I could hear myself screaming inside my head. I couldn't stop. I couldn't control anything at all, really. I didn't understand what was going on. It was the most terrifying, torturous feeling I have ever felt in my life. Each time I have a seizure, it gets scarier.

Twelve years, many seizures (including the worst day of my life when I had one at school in the tenth grade), and a lot of progress later, the possibility of having a seizure terrifies me on a daily basis. I have to take precautions in almost every aspect of my life to ensure that I can stay healthy and live a "normal" lifestyle. Did I take my medicine? Did I sleep eight hours? Will they want to go to a club or bar that has strobe lights? How do I tell everyone I can't go? Have I had enough to eat today?

Don't get me wrong, I have been fortunate in comparison to a lot of other epilepsy patients. I'm grateful for that, but these past twelve years have not been easy. I think "anxiety" is a bit of an understatement to describe the things my disease has done to me.

I was the only thirteen year old in the eighth grade with a "babysitter" of sorts. I was so embarrassed about not being able to stay home alone, but I had such bad anxiety attacks that I couldn't be left alone at all. What teenager doesn't want to stay home alone? One who is so terrified that she will have a seizure, bump her head, die alone, only to be found by her family hours later. Just the thought of having a seizure was enough to make me feel like my chest was collapsing and I was going to fall into a seizure at any moment.

The brain is such an amazing thing. I spent so much time calculating the possibilities of bad things that could happen to me that it left virtually no time for me to be a teenager. I couldn't breathe. I couldn't go to parties with strobe lights. I couldn't fully enjoy and experience the things I wanted to.

One thing that has truly helped me is comedy. Whether it was me making other people laugh or me laughing with people, it didn't matter. All I have ever really been good at is making people laugh. It is truly my favorite thing in the world to do.
I discovered my now-favorite social media application - Vine. My anxiety has greatly decreased and I've learned to cope over the years, and the comfort of laughing has never disappeared. The friends I have met on Vine have become amazing friends in real life and a big part of my life. We make each other laugh and share pieces of our lives. I am truly grateful for my new friendships.

You never know who you could be helping in a time they need it the most, and that makes it all worth it. I never thought complete strangers would tell me that my six-seconds of ridiculousness get them through a rough day.

## @Helenalovescake

I was born in Denmark and currently live there, and I suffer from schizotypal personality disorder. My mom and aunt also suffer from schizophrenia. I take medication and attend regular group therapy sessions.

I found Vine through The Ellen Show. I started vining for fun, without thinking about how many likes I'd get, but one day I decided to make a comedy vine. A few people noticed me. It made me really happy to know that people liked what I was doing. Soon, I made a video about my illness. Several people reached out to me and offered support.

Vine has helped me with my illness more than any other type of social media has. I have the freedom to be myself and forget about my illness and problems, even if only for a little while. Vine has allowed me to express myself in many ways, and it has made me feel brave.

I've made connections with people that would never have been possible outside Vine and I treasure every single friendship, every single day. I've talked to some of them in video chats, and it feels so natural and real, as if I've known them for ages. Vine is more than just an app to me. It's a place where I can talk and share my life with friends. Vine has helped me gain more confidence with my social skills. It has also helped me practice my English.

Downloading Vine is one of the best things I've ever done. I'm so glad I found it.

## *Anonymous Viner*

Last year, I was engaged to a woman who I was very much in love with. I found out that she was cheating on me. My world was shattered. I didn't eat. I didn't sleep. I began to have panic attacks whenever I would leave my house. As long as I stayed home, I didn't seem to have any panic attacks; however, I was usually anxious. I became a hermit. My life was boring.

A friend told me about Vine. I've always enjoyed making videos of myself acting silly so this was my kind of app. I started making vines and slowly but surely, people began to like my vines and tell me that I was funny. It was something that I needed at the time to take my mind from the anxiety and panic attacks. It gave me something to do while being stuck at home. Repeatedly, I found myself crying and depressed about the fact that I could not leave my apartment. I would go on Vine and see my favorite Viners, and it made me feel better.

So many of my friends on Vine know my story. Many of them also suffer from panic attacks and anxiety. I've lost so many real-life friends because of my condition. Because of Vine, I've gained many new friends. It's crazy how you can meet people through an app, and they become some of your closest friends. That's what I love most about this app.

Before Vine, I felt alone. I was suffering alone. The first time I made a vine about my agoraphobia, I received so many positive responses, which gave me so much confidence to try to get over my condition. I made a couple of vines of myself breaking down into tears while talking about how I couldn't take it anymore and that I was afraid I would do something I would regret.

That's when I met someone who is now one of my closest friends. She reached out to me that day and told me to contact her on Facebook. I connected with her and, basically, she talked me out of taking my own life. We now talk every day and she is honestly one of my best friends. I always wonder what would have happened if I had not made that vine. It was on that day that I realized that Vine is not just an app. There are people on Vine who actually care about me and want to help. So many people have befriended me. So many people are there for me.

I have been depressed so often, and all I have to do is watch a @Jeffrey Marsh vine and I feel like I'm not alone. Vine has helped me more than I could ever say.

## @Katieclemm

Have you ever had a feeling you just can't identify? You feel something, but you can't pinpoint it? Maybe you can identify the feeling as being one of emptiness, sadness, or anger, but you still don't understand why. You recognize that something is missing, but you can't draw the lines between the dots to see the big picture. I've lived with the feeling that something is missing for most of my life. I'm missing something, but I don't know what it is. The emptiness makes me sad. I have never understood what the problem is or what lies behind my unexplainable feelings.

I found that making me feel physical pain made my emotional pain less excruciating. Sometimes I was so drained that I couldn't feel anything at all. I wanted, I *needed* to feel. The razor blade became my best friend when I was about 12 years old. Lack of stability and abandonment from one of my parents played a role in my punishing myself. Cutting took the edge off. When I felt anxious, I would cut, and it helped ease those feelings.

I started college when I was sixteen years old. It was a lot of pressure, and I did the best I could to stay focused, but I felt alone. I thought there was no way that anyone could possibly understand me. I tried different things to keep myself from cutting such as rubber bands or holding ice cubes in my hands for long periods of time. Nothing was as good as a blade to my skin. My first trip to the hospital was when I was eighteen years old, and I had cut too deep. After many tears, seven staples, and a very long night in the hospital, I had never felt so defeated. I agreed to go to a counselor (which, by the way, didn't work out). Just like that, they let me go.

A year went by and after my third visit to the hospital for stitches, the emergency room staff were really getting very tired of seeing me. The doctor who always took care of me had a look of concern on her face as she sat down to talk to me. I promised to get help, and I followed through with it. I was admitted to an outpatient mental health facility. I was not happy about it, I wasn't comfortable talking, my anxiety was extremely high, and their scheduling sucked. I stuck with it anyway.

I am now twenty-one years old and I see a psychiatrist. I am not ashamed. I am not ashamed of my scars. I am not ashamed of who I am. Every day, I become a stronger person. I've learned that you can't fight everything on your own. I'm the most stubborn person I've ever met, and refusing help when it was offered to me was the worst thing I could have done. I still have urges to cut, but it is now a matter of letting go and asking for help.

My life before Vine was definitely not as interesting and entertaining as it is now. As far as social media, I used Tumblr the most. I used it as a blog, and I wrote about everything on an almost-daily basis. It was private with a password that only my doctor, psychologist, and a few close friends could get in. Tumblr was my outlet. I used Facebook to be social, but I didn't post anything too personal.

I started to vine in April 2013. My friend sent me a funny video that she made, and I thought, "Wow! That is so awesome! I want to do that!" I began by doing random, silly vines. Most of my posts were of me at work, trying to entertain myself. I saw other people's vines and was jealous because I could never figure out how to do any of the cool stuff that they were doing. My posts were just funny encounters I had with customers at work or myself being bored.

As time went on, I began to meet and interact with people on the app; many of whom are now are some of my closest friends. I started participating in hash tags and all the fun things that everyone else participated in. People started to like me! I could express myself however I wanted and still got positive comments.

From Vine, I get entertainment, laughter, hope, inspiration, friendship, and so much more. I never thought that downloading an app would mean so much to me. This app has changed my life. I hope that my vines make people smile. I often post "Never Lose Hope" vines, and I hope that people know that they aren't alone. I hope they know that things really do get better with time. I'm a friend to anyone who is willing to be a friend back, and I want to help them with whatever they are going through.

Vine has helped me stay focused. When I have bad days, I go on Vine. When I want to hurt myself, I go on Vine. I have used Vine to distract myself until the bad thoughts went away. I've made some close friends from the app whom I've grown to trust. I can text them and they are there for me. Vine has helped me and is still helping me get out of the darkness that I have been stuck in for so many years.

## @Kathrine Sullivan

My name is Kathrine Sullivan and I am 19 years old. I discovered Vine a few months ago through the guy I was dating at the time. I originally thought Vine was simply a way to pass time while watching other people having fun. I quickly realized that there was more to it. Vine has become a way for me to express myself. It has allowed me to share things that I thought I couldn't share with anyone.

I began cutting when I was in my freshman year of high school. When I cut, I black out and lose control. My father and I used to fight a lot when I was in school. We still do. My lack of a social network was also a major contributor. Really, I had no life. I got bullied a lot, and my way of dealing with it was to seclude myself from everyone. To add to my pain, I had recently broken up with someone. I was left feeling as though the world had given up on me. I believed that there was no point in life anymore.

When I broke my one-year sobriety from cutting, I realized Vine was a way to seek help. I saw it as a way to reach out for support and develop new relationships. There are Viners who have helped me through a lot without even realizing that they were doing so. One of the Viners who helped me the most is @Wesley Besides. I love his vines. He is the sweetest man I have ever met. If I ever needed a laugh, just watching a Logan Paul or Jen Dent vine would help brighten my day. These things may seem very small or meaningless to many people, but they have impacted my life in so many positive ways. I'm so thankful that I downloaded Vine.

# Seven

# Chronic Illness

*@goldenbee*

Vine has been such an amazing, positive, and uplifting outlet for so many people. I have found that most Viners are like-minded, creative people looking to laugh and feel good about life.

I have a congenital medical condition, and I have given myself the title of "Professional Patient". I have a lot of free time due to prescribed bed rest, and I find myself on my phone quite a bit as a distraction. I downloaded Vine on the day that it launched. My anxiety often increases when I gain new followers. I feel that there is danger in numbers: more followers mean more creeps, mean people, and spambots. On the positive side, I have made many amazing friends through Vine. It has enriched my life.

I find Vine to be very positive. If anyone is negative, other people are quick to react and remind them of their humanity and humility. Vine is a family of people who stick up for each other, and I feel blessed to be part of it.

There are many smart, witty, talented, and awesome people on Vine. I try to be very real, open, and relatable in my vines. I revine things that I find entertaining, I don't keep track of my followers, and I treat Vine as a way to have fun and to let loose. I control my Vine feed. I block people if I feel as though it's necessary.

I created the hash tag #KEEPVINEPOSITIVE. I'm proud of that. I also created #BeesStomachSucks about a month after creating my Vine account. Now, I can go back and see myself fluctuate 30 lbs, see myself being admitted and discharged from the hospital, have heart procedures, get PICC lines, cry, and laugh. Those things are all part of my journey. Six seconds isn't much time, but it's just enough for me. I think of it as a perfect filter through which I can view the history of my life.

## @Sydney Rohmann

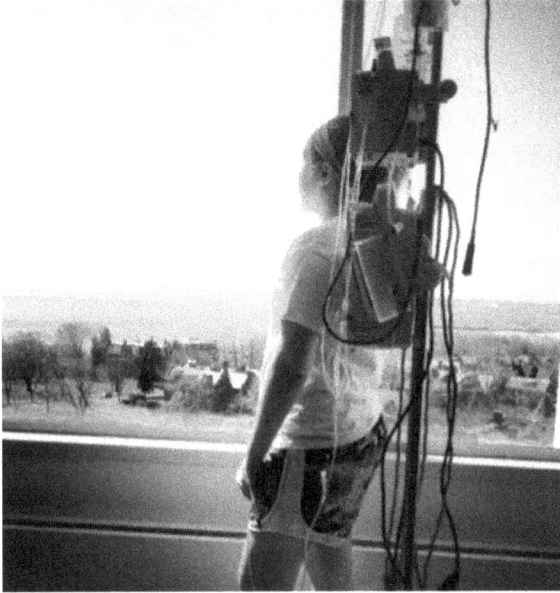

*Interview conducted with permission of Sherry Rohmann.*

I am 17 years old and a senior in high school. During the summer of 2012, I became very ill. I had really bad pain in the back of my head. My family doctor sent me to an ear specialist, and I had ear surgery, but it did not relieve the pain.

I was then sent to a neurologist. Again, I found no relief, as nothing helped. During the month of October, I was in the Emergency Room at least three times a week. I had a second MRI, and on November 15th, 2012, I was finally diagnosed with chiari malformation, a condition in which your brain sags down into your spinal cord.

This condition causes many health problems, one of which is severe pain. Brain surgery is an option but not a cure. My symptoms continually worsened. I even went deaf in my left ear. I spent many months going in and out of the hospital, which caused me to miss my entire junior year of high school. The neurosurgeon was uncomfortable performing surgery due to my age. I spent four more months going from doctor to doctor, hospital to hospital, and receiving multiple unhelpful treatments. Finally, I found a doctor who said he would perform the surgery I needed.

On April 1, 2013, I had brain surgery. It lasted four hours, and I was in the hospital for a week. The healing process was long, but it was well worth it. Many of my symptoms went away. My hearing came back. I had some complications after surgery, like bad headaches, but they eventually went away. I had a great summer, with some random bad days thrown in. Mostly I felt great, but in August, I started to feel sick again.

Ever since August of 2013, I have had the same symptoms that I had before my surgery. My doctors tell me that they don't know what's going on. I am on many drugs and being passed from one doctor to another. This has made attending school very difficult. Giving up hope has seemed like an option at times, but I have never chosen to do so.

I downloaded Vine in April 2013, but didn't really interact with other people until August. I began to realize that all Viners were on the app to find other people to relate to and I made many friends. Vine has changed me. @goldenbee reminds me that I am not alone. I see people on Vine deal with daily struggles, even if they aren't health-related. Everyone has their own rough patches in life, and Vine has helped me remember that.

Vine has also shown me that I don't have to change to fit in. I can just be myself and people will like me no matter what. I am open with my life struggles. Watching my story has helped others. My illness has changed me, but I have tried to make sure that the change is a positive one. I want to be a better person. I want to make people smile and laugh. Even if I am having bad day, maybe I can help someone else have a good one because of my vines. That would mean the world to me.

# @Scar-Let Roo and @SteveR

### *Scar-let Roo:*

I have the third rarest autoimmune disease in the country. It is Dercums disease type three, otherwise known as adiposis dolorosa. Two years ago, I developed tremors and the doctors thought I may have had multiple sclerosis, but my MRI was normal.

Last March, the tremor had spread throughout my body. I had doubled and blurred vision, slurred speech, and difficulties with swallowing and breathing. Again, the doctors thought it was multiple sclerosis, but after lots of testing they determined that it was an autoimmune disease called myasthenia gravis, which translates to "grave muscle weakness". With this disease, your brain does not communicate normally with your muscles.

On top of these two autoimmune diseases, I will have had nineteen surgeries since the age of twenty. The operations range from back surgeries, infertility surgeries, organ removal, tumor removal, sinus surgery, eye surgery, dercums disease fat removal surgeries, and a breast cancer scare surgery that was then followed by three reconstructive surgeries.

Vine helps me because I am home bound. I haven't been able to drive for over a year, and I'm bedridden much of the time. I get bored, and I have no outlet or social life, most of the time. Vine helps me feel somewhat normal. It gives me a chance to socialize with people and gives me a chance to still be myself without having to leave the house.

*SteveR:*

If lightning can hit the same person twice, it would hit Scar-Let. We've been dealing with her chronic conditions since she was twenty years old.

She had a big tumor removed from between her lungs last July. She was doing well with her recovery until she fell while making a vine, of all things. She broke one of the discs in her spine. She had already undergone two previous back surgeries and had to have yet another one due to her fall.

Vine is kind of like Facebook for Scar-Let, but better. She creates a lot of abstract art. With Facebook, she can connect with other people, and while that is important, she has developed her own little Vine family. She's part of a community on Vine.

Vine is a way for her to have fun. Watching her vines, you would never know that Scar-Let is in constant pain. I like seeing her make vines while I'm at my office. I worry about her when I am at work, but when I see that she has made a vine it gives me some reassurance that she is okay.

# @MARLINSMÆSH

I live in British Columbia, Canada. I was formerly the director of a provincial employment program for a Native American organization of which I am also a citizen. When I was forty-three, I had a massive stroke brought on by poor living, obesity, severe hypertension, and stress. I developed a right hemisphere hypertensive bleed in the basal ganglia area of my brain. Upon admission to the emergency room, I was paralyzed on my left side, and my blood pressure reading had skyrocketed. The physicians gave me a 50/50 chance of living through the night.

I recovered and was released ten days later, but I was still partially paralyzed. I left the hospital with severely debilitating and underlying mental, emotional, and physical conditions. I had difficulties with my speech. It was hard to speak even a few words. My brain knew the words but couldn't seem to communicate with my mouth. When it did work, my mouth couldn't form the words without stuttering. I also had an extreme short-term memory deficit and problems with concentration.

I sought out traditional therapies, but soon realized that most of them are geared towards older stroke patients. Instead, I played Wii video games and iPhone-based programs to assist in retraining my brain by using neuroplasticity techniques. I discovered Vine in January 2013, soon after it was launched. I found that I could use it to help with my socialization skills and speech difficulties.

At first, my vines were just pictures as it was very difficult for me to speak. The fact that I could re-shoot videos repeatedly made it seem as though I spoke well, but the fifteen outtakes told a different story. The six-second window of Vine was perfect for me due to my short-term memory.

As I gained confidence, my speech improved. Listening to my own vines and hearing myself speak well also increased my confidence. My vines grew more complicated, and I gained even more confidence. At first, I had to use words that I could pronounce easily. Eventually, I took part in a collaboration involving superhero stories, which led to creating my own collaboration account with a fake news-style network.

Today, I speak almost perfectly on Vine. I couldn't do these things nine months ago. I have branched out and socialized on other social media apps, and most people cannot tell that only two years ago I could hardly talk. My personal physician and neurologist are amazed with my progress. Vine has definitely helped me in my recent personal victories.

## @NeenBean

I'm not an avid poster on Vine, but I am an observer and I follow Viners who inspire me by making me laugh or standing up for causes I, myself, believe in. I turn to Vine during times of stress, vacancy, or chaos in my life and it's also a great distraction for when I have to wait in doctors' offices, wait for stomach pains to stop, or to wait for my school grades to come back. I seem to always be waiting for things. Vine calms me and gives me something else to focus on, even if it is only a temporary distraction. I find solace in it.

The escape I've found through Vine has helped me cope with my depression and it's helped me move through some difficult patches with my Crohn's disease. It helps to know that there's a community of people on Vine who experience the exact same issues that I do. When my stress is relieved, my quality of life improves, my condition doesn't flare, and I cope better with my depression.

I realized that Vine was more than just short videos when I discovered other Viners who have Crohn's. I found a network of people who were experiencing exactly what I was going through. Some of them have had it longer, and have more severe cases.

Others are just as new to the disease as I. It meant a lot to me that people were sharing their struggles, and it showed me that I am not alone.

It is very interesting to me that we all live in vastly different areas, have different life experiences, and have grown in different cultures, yet we have a community on Vine, a personal connection. Vine gives us a glimpse into the lives of those who would be otherwise strangers.

# @Shae Haskins

My name is Shae Haskins, and I'm seventeen years old. I'm your typical teenage girl except for one thing: I have a disorder known for being one of the most painful diseases called complex regional pain syndrome (CRPS). A doctor told me, "If hell were a disease, CRPS would be it".

CRPS is a rare, aggressive, progressive, and degenerative neurological nerve disorder. It is the result of an event that your body views as traumatic, such as an accident or a medical procedure. Years ago, I broke my arm four times and had one surgery. A few years later, my CRPS activated. When a limb is injured, your sympathetic nervous system is activated, and then calmed within ten to thirty minutes. CRPS develops when this sympathetic nervous system never calms, and causes the limb to be red, swollen, and hot to the touch.

The brain of a CRPS patient constantly thinks it is still injured after the injury has long been healed. The pain experienced by CRPS is not equivalent to the initial injury; rather, it is much worse. Many health professionals say that it is the worst pain a person can endure, topping childbirth and amputation. Daily activities become extremely difficult due to the affected limb being constantly bumped or touched; even a fan on in a room can cause pain.

There is no cure for CRPS, and the few treatment options available can be very invasive or damaging. The medications can be damaging to the liver, and most patients report very little help from the medications at all.

I have to undergo outpatient procedures every few weeks and receive nerve blocks. I am constantly in and out of physical and occupational therapy, trying to combat this extremely aggressive disorder.

No thanks to CRPS, I have severe tremors in my hand, and I have developed a contracture in that hand. Because of those two things, I cannot write. I essentially have one arm because the disease has caused so much degeneration in the right one, that I have little use of it. It also causes extreme fatigue. Taking a shower or walking up the stairs can seem like impossible tasks.

Recently, my doctors discovered that I have stage four CRPS, in which my internal organs have also been affected. My gastrointestinal tract has been damaged, so I am no longer able to eat or drink anything. I have constant, severe abdominal pain and nausea. If I eat or drink anything my stomach bloats as though I have swallowed a watermelon whole. I also suffer from constant dizziness, frequent fainting spells, severe joint pain, thermal regulation issues, rapid pulse, and more.

I am very sick, but some positive things have come out of it. I found an outlet, a place that was a safe haven for me. I connected with other people who had CRPS or chronic illnesses who could relate to what I was going through. They completely understood what it was like to be sick.

A seemingly ordinary app called Vine allowed me to find people who understood and didn't judge me. It showed me how much support I really have in my fight for my health and it has helped me to keep going and stay positive.

When you are diagnosed with a rare disease, you feel completely and utterly alone. All you want is to connect and talk to other people who are experiencing the same issue so you have a support system. I found my place. Vine really changed my life. I've received so much support and love.

Vine is home. Vine is a major part of my support system. Vine taught me that it is okay that I'm sick and that I shouldn't feel as though I have to hide it from anyone. After I was diagnosed, my world turned upside down. When I started vining, it was the first time that I felt normal in a long time.

## @*Melissa Glitter*

**"272,160,000 Seconds, Give Or Take a Few"**

Every night, I pull a blanket over my very well fed Basset, Waylon, kiss him on his wrinkled, very slobber-ridden forehead, and say the same thing. "Tomorrow will be a better day that we won't take for granted." I feel as though I am the only thirty-two year-old woman tucking her dog in, instead of her children or companion. I also feel lucky and extremely blessed to be able to do this alone, and not with the help of an aide. This isn't a story about how I feel; it's a story about how six seconds made a difference in my life more than any publication, advice, or alternative treatment within the last nine years.

July 24, 2005. I remember the smell of the room, the tired look in my Mom's eyes, the clothes I was wearing, and most importantly, the look of sympathy on my doctor's face when he said the four words that would change my life forever: "You have Multiple Sclerosis."

I went to a support group, and I was the youngest person there by at least thirty years. I read everything I could on the Internet about my diagnosis. I went to MS Society events where I was considered "skank-faced" for having tattoos and pink hair. I raised money, donated money, and assembled the largest of the participating teams for annual walks for awareness in my hometown. I heard whispers and saw stares of judgment not only for me but also for the friends who stood by my side. None of those things worked for me, and I gave up. I decided that from now on, I would hide not only the diagnosis but also my charitable efforts. I would have to raise awareness anonymously.

Only a handful of people knew my secret. Some called it strength, but I called it "being stubborn." I continued the daily struggle of waking up with no feeling in my legs or hands. I was so fatigued that I would have to sit down in the shower because it took so much energy just to wash my hair. I dealt with constantly urinating myself in public, paralysis in my face, forgetting if I brushed my teeth or sometimes even brushing them with lotion. I dealt with mental issues, such as memory loss and depression.

As the years went by, I found myself becoming more and more withdrawn from the outside world. The only social interactions I maintained were when I was at work. I sat at home most days ignoring calls and texts from friends. I didn't want to tell them that I didn't feel well. I was angry that I felt that way, but I did it to myself. I hid this from almost everyone, and even the people who knew my struggles didn't know much.

"You should download Vine," a customer urged in late summer of 2013, and I did. I made a few of my own, but I mostly just watched. I found a Viner and watched all of her vines from the very beginning. I wanted to be friends with her in real life. I saw how much hate she got, and I didn't understand why. I commented, "For what it's worth, I know my opinion doesn't matter but I think you're amazing."

She responded, "Melissa Glitter, everyone matters." Wow, I have ten spambot followers, and she has over 30,000 and she answered me. I knew she didn't know my struggle, or ho I was, but I knew how great that felt to be told that I mattered.

In October, I started vining every day. I was so happy to be able to be myself instead of that person who had to be a fake for fear of losing friends in real life. At the end of October, someone made a comment on a vine mocking my face. I knew they didn't know about my MS, but it still made me cry. I made a vine during one of my monthly infusion treatments and tagged it #multiplesclerosis. I had never mentioned MS on social media since being diagnosed, and this was a big step for me. I made another vine pausing on a paper telling my story. Afterwards, people began to contact me about MS.

I began offering advice and encouragement and people thanked me for talking about it.
I felt like a sham. I had hidden this from people in my personal life. I felt more comfortable telling a phone my problems. On the other hand, I began to see that I was accomplishing what I had always wanted to do: Raising awareness, not judgment.

March is MS Awareness month. At the beginning of March, I made a vine, and showed my brain scans to the outside world for the first time. I used the hash tag #MSawareness and soon had Viners with huge follower counts making vines for the cause. Within the first week of March, over one hundred Viners made awareness vines. I was so humbled and proud. People began to thank me for doing this for us. *US*. People began to count on me to fight for awareness.

On March 9, 2014, I made a vine about the end of Awareness week. This was the first time that the words came out of my mouth: "I have MS."

I cried while uploading the vine. On that day, I had been diagnosed for 272,160,000 seconds, give or take a few and all it took were six seconds to feel more alive and encouraged than ever. I am not ready to shout it from the rooftops just yet, but I am done hiding. If I don't feel well I will tell you. How can I ask for you to not judge me when that's exactly what I am doing by not being honest?

This is not the end of my story. It's just the beginning. I will add more chapters about the amazing friendships I have made with other Viners, one of whom gives me the most encouragement, and shares the same name as a fruit; and how I fell in love with a man from another country.

When my story is complete, I will have Vine to thank for helping me change my life and giving me encouragement.

*@NadineLove*

I have been sick for a while, as well as depressed. I was born with Neurofibrometosis, which is a disease that causes tumors to grow on my nerves. At the age of nineteen, I was diagnosed with Hashimoto's, a thyroid disease that causes fatigue, depression, and muscle pain.

I downloaded Vine on October 28, 2013. First, all I did was observe. I have been socially awkward since I left school due to bullying. For almost a week, I didn't post very much. I didn't show myself in any of them. After a week of doing that, I made some posts of myself but I was very quiet and timid. After a few weeks, I began to interact with other Viners and make some new friends. I saw a glimpse of the compassion that these people had.

I was very sick from starting some new medications. I felt very run down and tired. My hair started falling out. A new friend that I met made a few vines for me, and even made a hash tag in my honor. I started to realize what an impact Vine had. I began to get more and more comfortable. I began to speak louder and I began making vines for other people, reaching out and trying to make other people smile.

Even if I was having a bad day and made a vine for someone else, it made me feel good to know that I made that person happy. I began to feel really good about myself.

My grandmother passed away on the morning after Christmas. I have never received so much love and support as I did that day and the week to follow. People I didn't even know reached out to me. They sent me messages. A couple of people even sent me cards and some flowers. No one in my life outside of Vine had reached out to me; yet, strangers on an app were there for me. On that day, I realized that there are many amazing people in the world. There are so many wonderful people on Vine. On my bad days, there are certain people whose Vine pages I go to and can't help smiling. Even if I've watched their vines 1,000 times already, watching them again brings me such joy and makes me feel so much better.

I've been posting my health journey on Vine. This is not just an app to me. I think that without Vine, I would be much worse off than I was before. To have this community and family online, when you don't feel as though you have it in your real life, is hard to explain to someone who has not experienced it. People who haven't used Vine or gotten into the community aspect of it wouldn't understand the connections, compassion, and love that you get from these little six-second videos.

Vine has shown me that I am not alone and that I am loved.

*Eight*

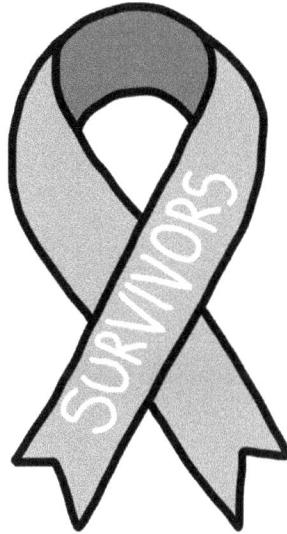

*Survivors*

**NOTE:** *This chapter contains graphic descriptions of violence and rape. Reader discretion is advised.*

*@Jen Dent*

I have always been aware of the term "rape culture" and how rape victims were and still are shamed in our society. It wasn't until recently that I saw it firsthand. What I have witnessed in the last few months has left me astounded and appalled. The Vine community that I grew to love and cherish has let women down in so many ways. While I still love the app and always will, it's hard to look past the awful things I have seen happen.

Feminists started using the term "rape culture" in the 1970s. Many women viewed sexual assault as inevitable. Many women expected to be violated at least once in their lives and took it upon themselves to avoid rape at all costs. Many wore panty hose that made them appear to have hairy legs, to be perceived as unattractive and "not worthy of rape". Some women left their homes with anti-rape condoms inserted into their vaginas. These condoms had jagged teeth designed to tear a man's penis if he penetrated her against her will. Take note: Women were taught to *try to avoid being raped*, but men were *not* taught *not to rape*. The term "Rape Culture" means that it is a woman's job to defend herself against rape always.

When I was about 26 years old, my partner at the time and I went to a party, and I got pretty drunk. When we got home, I hurriedly changed into my pajamas, brushed my teeth, and went to bed. My partner also got into bed and immediately began to try to have sex with me. I told him that I was drunk, tired, and on my period. He sulked a bit, but I didn't give in. All I wanted to do was sleep. I'm not sure how much later it was when I woke up under him as he was having sex with me. I was confused at first. That confusion quickly turned into fear.

"What are you doing? I have a tampon in," I said.

Disgusted, yet not getting off me, he told me that I was so "fucking drunk" that I didn't remember getting up and taking it out. I instantly felt shame for being so drunk and forgetful. I lay there as he finished having sex with me. When he was done, I went back to sleep. The next morning, I found my tampon lying on the floor on his side of the bed. I walked into the living room and confronted him. "You said I got up and took this out," I said, holding the tampon out for him to see.

He just shrugged and continued watching TV.

The next day, I told a coworker about it. She stood there with her mouth gaped open as I talked. When I was done, she said, "So he raped you. You know that, right?"

No. I did not know that. I didn't realize that someone who you were in a relationship with could rape you. After all, we had already had sex and were living together. How could that be rape?

Eventually, and for many more reasons, I left him.

What is rape? According to many sources, rape is forced sexual intercourse, including anal, vaginal, or oral penetration. Penetration may be by a body part or an object. Sexual assault is unwanted sexual contact that stops short of rape or attempted rape. This includes sexual touching and fondling.

In order for sex to be consensual, the people engaging in the sex act must be of legal age of consent in that state or country. For someone to consent to sex, they must be mentally capable of doing so. If a person is of diminished mental capacity, he or she cannot legally consent. Diminished mental capacity encompasses a wide range of scenarios including, but not limited to, being drugged, asleep, or unconscious. Lastly, both people must have agreed to have sex. If both people have agreed, the sex has already begun, and then one of the people decides they don't want to continue; it must stop. If it does not, the sex is no longer consensual and is therefore rape. According to these definitions and guidelines, I was indeed raped.

Jessi Smiles has become one of my closest friends. The first time I ever spoke with her on Vine, my Gramma had just passed away, and my sister and I were drinking. I got on Vine and saw Jessi celebrating one million followers. Being sad, angry, and a little drunk, I made a smart-ass comment. She blocked me. Ironically, several weeks later, she started following me. I wanted to follow her back, but I couldn't because I was blocked. I told her I was blocked, explained why, and apologized. She immediately accepted my apology and we've been friends ever since.

Jessi told me her story one night in October 2013. We hardly knew each other at the time, and the circumstances surrounding that evening were strange. Somehow, I ended up on the phone with her and suddenly she was sharing details with me that I was unprepared to hear. If you aren't aware of her story, google "Jessi Smiles" to learn what happened. I had never really talked about what happened to me before she shared her story. When she did, it was like a candle that had been extinguished for 14 years inside a tiny little room in my mind was finally lit. Not only was it lit, but it grew into an out of control fire, engulfing everything around it in flames. I know it was not evident to anyone else involved in the conversation, but I felt as if I had been slapped across the face, being told to wake up. Finally, Jen. Wake the fuck up.

On the day that TMZ published the story about Jessi Smiles, I shared my story on Vine. I knew that people were going to call her a liar because although they were no longer a couple when the incident took place, she had dated her offender. In an attempt to show solidarity, I came forward. I was greeted with a barrage of insults.

*"How can someone rape you if you are in a relationship? When you live with somebody it means you're down to fuck whenever."*

*"You should be ashamed of yourself that you got that drunk in the first place."*

*"Shut up, that's not rape. You're just being dramatic and want attention."*

I have been very vocal about her situation. I have been accused of talking about it for attention. People say I involved myself to gain followers. In reality, I lost about 5,000 followers from taking a stance on the issue. People who I really liked stopped talking to me. I've been told that I make people uncomfortable because I talk about rape. I've also been attacked, receiving threats of death, physical violence, rape, financial hacking, and social media hacking.

People told me that I needed to be funny and make people laugh instead of talking about a real problem that exists and happens every day all over the world. I've clicked on vines made by people who I thought liked me, only to see that they were bashing me. Why? They didn't want to see the "drama" on my page. I was "leading a hate campaign". I've read comments from people saying that I didn't handle this the correct way. My response is simple. At least I did something. At least I said something. Most of the people who judge me haven't done or said anything. Perhaps they said something behind the scenes, but never where it really mattered.

I've been volunteering with the Family Violence and Sexual Assault Unit (FVSAU, @FVSAU on Vine) in my hometown for about five years. I'm well aware of the horrific things that happen to women in this world. Watching Jessi get attacked on Vine by hundreds of people and vilified was just another example of how women are abused and then disrespected. I have helped with our annual fundraiser every April. I even got attacked for that on Vine recently. I really think people just sit around and get angry with other people for doing good things. They don't like to see other people receive positive attention.

I talked about the situation. Too much. I went overboard. I was downright manic some days, but this is important to me. Why is it okay for people to do hash tags and loops all day long, but it's not okay for me to talk about rape? To them, I have let something that is important to me "overshadow my comedy".

I've been asked why I talk about it. Why do I want to make people "uncomfortable"? People ask me why I am worried about it when it didn't happen to me. Well, why do people talk about cancer? Why do people talk about starving children? Why do people talk about soldiers at war? Why do people talk about animal abuse? Why do we talk about those things if they didn't happen to us?

The reason is that it is every person's responsibility to speak up when they see that a human being has been wronged. More importantly, it is every woman's responsibility to stand up for her fellow woman. I have been completely floored by the misogyny that I've seen from females on Vine toward Jessi and myself. The comments have amazed me, and not in a good way. I would blame it all on the children who are not supposed to be on the app in the first place, but unfortunately, adult women have been just as bad.

There are so many things I will never understand about human nature, but I *do* understand this:

I have a responsibility to use my Vine platform in ways that will educate people. To sit back and be silent doesn't help anything or anyone. For this reason, I have taken on new responsibilities: I will be doing more than fundraising once a year for FVSAU from now on, and I will be volunteering one day a week with the organization. I begin my training soon, which involves going to court with the director of the program and learning the process. Eventually, I will be working one-on-one with the victims and survivors, mainly going with them to trials and hearings.

The most recent FVSAU annual fundraiser was held on April 5, 2014. Ameera Belle, Ben Talley, and Christina Nicole XO, Viners from New York City, volunteered to come to Virginia and help. Another Viner, Blake Cook, came from South Carolina. None of them asked for anything in return. Jessi also came from Miami, surprising me after she and my husband kept the visit a secret from me for three weeks.

Using Vine, we raised more money for violence and sexual assault survivors than the organization has received since it began in 1991. It was a very emotional night filled with happiness, sadness, and a sense of family. My little hometown knows what Vine is now. They see us as inspirations. They see us as people who stick together and get things done. Had it not been for Vine, this year would not have been as successful as it was. So, really, Vine hasn't let women down at all. It has helped in ways that I didn't think were possible or even imaginable.

I want to thank Jessi Smiles for trusting me and for comforting me when I needed it, even when she was going through hell herself. As cliché as it sounds, I want to thank the people who turned against me. I want to thank the people who actually attacked me for standing my ground, just making me stronger. For every person who treated me like shit, there are five more people who supported me and thanked me for standing up and speaking out. Those are the people that I will never forget.

Vine is not just for fun. Vine is what we make it. Sometimes life isn't fun. That's just how it is. I don't regret anything I have said or done.

# @*Jessi Smiles*

I used to do song covers, parodies, and makeup tutorials on YouTube. I loved drama class in high school, and I liked to express myself in creative ways. When I look back at them, it's painfully evident how awkward I was. I looked so weird trying to connect with the camera and the audience. I've changed so much since then.

I started using Vine near the end of May 2013. The first few vines I did were of my cat or me and my friends sitting by the pool acting silly. I immediately started watching the Popular Now page and laughing. It didn't take long for me to begin making my own comedy vines.

What I liked about Vine at that time, was the community. There were nowhere near as many people on the app as there are now. It was such a warm and supportive place. There were never any hate comments, and everything was positive and encouraging. I remember feeling that I was so lucky to have found a place like Vine. It was a place where I found people like me: People who liked to express themselves and accept others to do the same.

By the beginning of August 2013, I had one million followers and became Vine verified. It happened so fast. I began to see the "other side of Vine". There is a lot more to Vine than people know. It was very exciting for me at first, but I quickly learned that dealing with that other side would ruin the feelings I had for the app.

Lately, I haven't enjoyed Vine like I used to. I don't feel the joy that I used to feel when I made vines. The experience is nothing like it used to be. It's worse and it's better at the same time. There is a lot of negativity, but at the same time, there are positive pieces that will stay with me forever.

On a day when I was feeling particularly down, all the people leaving negative comments were doing just that: Leaving comments and going on about their business. There were, however, people who outshined those negative people drastically. They outshined them more than I could have ever imagined in my life. They were taking time out of their day to make vines for me. They took six seconds of their day to encourage me, to send me love, and to comfort me. I saw pure love that day. There are no words to explain how much I needed that and how much it meant to me. It still means so much. Although I don't post that much anymore, I'm still on Vine every day. I don't go to the Popular Now page, and I don't look at the profiles of the better-known Viners. Instead, I check out my friends' vines. If they revine something that I think is funny, I go look at that person's profile. Something that makes me feel excited and special is when I go to someone's profile and see that they are following me. Even after 3 million followers, I still get a happy feeling when I see that another creative person finds me worth following.

People have a way of backing you into a corner and making you turn on what you believe. Forget those people. It's sad to say this, but all we have is our truth: What we know. What we believe to be 100% true. We have to learn to believe in and not doubt ourselves simply because of the doubts of others. It's hard. People have backed me into a corner and made me question myself a million times. Don't let people tell you that you can't or shouldn't do what you believe in. It's your life. It's your Vine. Remember that.

Although I'm not on Vine as much as before, I still check in. And I still recognize that because of this app my life has changed so much for the better.

### @*Joshua of Grand Rapids*

I'm missing almost a year of my life. I didn't remember my attack until I was in my twenties, but that doesn't mean it didn't affect my life before then (I'm a sexual anorexic). What it does mean is that I'll never be able to press charges against my rapist. I don't remember his name. Given the span between what happened and my conscious recollection of it, it's very likely that no one would be willing to hear my case anyway.

The only real way for me to feel in control is to speak out; however, this has always been difficult. Being male and identifying as a man, I'm privileged, meaning I'm less likely to be dismissed, but I *am* more likely to have my story met with disbelief. I'm not the type of person with whom society has been trained to picture as a victim. Given my gender, along with the twenty plus years between what happened and today, it's also very likely that people will tell me to "get over it". Anyone who knows what it's like to be a survivor knows it's impossible to get over. It has changed how I perceive things, how I interact with people, and how I process my relationships and sexuality. "Getting over it" would require a paradigm shift in my personality. This is something that I can only expect other survivors to understand.

Speaking about my experiences and how they've affected my life was something largely restricted to formats in which I could be anonymous. I became very involved in the social justice community on Tumblr. I'd spent much time blogging about sexual justice, gender equality, and other issues that impact the lives of survivors. The anonymity mostly kept me safe, mostly. People knew I was a man, that I was white and that I was basically straight, but they knew these details on a basis of privilege. I chose what I did and did not divulge. I still had a screen of privacy that allowed things to remain comfortable. I was, generally, in control.

The anonymity afforded to me by Tumblr ended up being so counterproductive that I found myself with my gun trained on my own head in March of 2013. My roommate came home, and I hid the gun to avoid my awkwardness. I had lined the windows of my car with cardboard and if he had not come home when he did, I would have taken the pistol out to my car and pulled the trigger. I removed the rounds from my revolver, closed my Tumblr account, and sought more positive ways to interact. Without the intent of it becoming as large a part of my life as it had, I downloaded the Vine app onto my phone in June.

As I developed relationships with other Viners and began to gain some followers, I started to feel the itch to talk about my mental health and my experience as a survivor. The inherently open and personal nature of Vine, however, made me apprehensive. I simply lacked the courage to talk publicly in a less-than-anonymous format.

In January, when Jessi Smiles' story was broken by TMZ, I felt more compelled. She didn't have the privilege of choosing how the world heard her story. I felt ethically compelled to show solidarity. I knew that I did not have the face of a typical rape survivor, but I knew that people might be a little more likely to take pause and think about an often intentionally ignored issue. Vine was still, however, a place for faces and I found it difficult to gather the courage I needed to come forward.

Then, Jen Dent came forward. She had 30 times the followers I had. She, with her refusal to play doormat to others, is a very polarizing personality in the Vine community. I knew there were many people who did not like her. If she had the courage to share her experience with all the negativity she was sure to face, I knew I had to, as well. I felt that I'd be disrespecting other survivors if I didn't. I'd be disrespecting her if I didn't. I'd be disrespecting my sister (also a survivor) if I didn't. Thanks to Jen's courage, I finally realized how much I'd be disrespecting myself if I didn't. Coming forward on Vine as a survivor was one of the most emotionally difficult experiences of my life. It was also one of the most emotionally rewarding.

I have plenty of friends in the real world. Most of them know that I'm a survivor, and they support me. On the day I came forward, however, I found myself relying more on the people I've grown close to through Vine for support. The friendships I've founded through this little app, this social network, have been some of the fastest and most deeply bonded friendships I've ever had. I know I am not the only one who feels this way.

I'd hardly call myself an idealist, but Vine may be at the event horizon of a massive awareness to cultural diseases, like rape. That makes it a community that is more than special: That makes it a movement. That makes all the fear, loathing, and depression "worth it." If nothing else, it is definitely more effective in easing the feeling of loneliness than a circle of chairs in a private community center room.

# @Roseanne Barr

*Interview with Roseanne Barr by Jen Dent*

*Roseanne Barr is an actress, comedian, writer, producer, director, and 2012 presidential nominee for the Peace and Freedom Party of California. She began her career as a stand-up comedian and soon had her own television sitcom, "Roseanne", which ran from 1988 to 1997. She won an Emmy, a Golden Globe, a Kids Choice Award, and three American Comedy Awards for her performance on the show.*

*She is known for portraying a "fierce, working-class domestic goddess" in those 9 years of her sitcom. She has also written several books, appeared in films in both acting and voiceover work, acted in stage productions, and starred in both her own talk show and reality show. She has hosted Saturday Night Live three times. She was the first female comedian to host The MTV Movie Awards in 1994 and remained the only female to do so until Chelsea Handler hosted in 2010.*

*Currently, Roseanne is working on multiple projects and lives on a macadamia farm in Hawaii. You can find her Twitter as @TheRealRoseanne.*

*Because of recent events on Vine, I wanted to talk to her about being outspoken and taking a stand when you believe in something, despite the result. She was very generous in answering all my questions.*

**JD: Hi Roseanne. I see that you have always been outspoken throughout your career, most recently on Twitter. I consider you as a role model, and I have been using you as an example of strength in the last few weeks. Have you always been this outspoken? And if so, why?**

RB: Yes. I was born this way. It's because I grew up Jewish in an apartment building filled with Holocaust survivors, sponsored by my grandparents in Salt Lake City, Utah.

**JD: How did you become so comfortable in not giving a fuck?**

RB: I fight Nazis on every level every day. It gives me great pleasure to do so.

**JD: Do you ever second-guess yourself after you have spoken out about something?**

RB: Of course. It's scary to step out of the pack.

**JD: How does it affect you when someone tells you that you are wrong for speaking out? If so, how?**

RB: I'm a comedian, so I like to decode bullshit and write about forbidden subjects. It angers me that people think they can bully, harass, and oppress people who don't think the same way they do. Anger is a great battery, especially righteous anger.

It's actually kind of hilarious in a dark way that mind-controlled slaves attack truth, though they are largely incapable of ascertaining or recognizing it. They operate on emotion only because they are incapable of having genuine thoughts.

**JD:  Are there differences in how outspoken women are treated in comparison with outspoken men? If so, what are the differences?**

RB:  Yes. Women rush to defend men, no matter how repulsive their ideals are. Women also rush to silence women who are braver than they are, or who speak about fact instead of stereotypical gender assumptions. For doing these things, women are held up as "virtuous" when they are actually traitors and imbeciles.

Men don't understand most of what any woman says because they are raised to have no empathy for the plight of the world's women. I rarely see an outspoken man. They are mostly arrogant narcissists who regurgitate some party line for personal reward, or to curry favor in one male Mafia or another. To most men, women are talking cows.

*Note from Jen Dent:  (The following Vine comments were sent to Roseanne prior to the interview)*

*Name withheld [female]:  "The 'rape' apparently happened in August...she filed the report in October...uhhhh????sketch"*

*Name withheld [female]:  "Plus how could she know she was raped if she was unconscious...I don't get it."*

*Name withheld [male]:  "Lmfao yo (name withheld) why she dancing for?"*

*Name withheld [male]:  "Stop lying you attention WHORE!"*

*Name withheld [female]:  "(name withheld) is a liar."*

*Name withheld [female]:  "(name withheld) raped you? Ha, yeah right, attention whore."*

*Name withheld [male]: "Ain't rape if a hoe says yes."*

*Name withheld [female]: "You don't know what rape is so don't go around saying you were, lying lying lyingggggggg."*

*Name withheld [female]: "Attention whore. Get the fuck over yourself. So many more people are on 'team (name withheld). You just lost a fuck ton of fans."*

RB: How they are different depends on the subject. I'm sick and tired of women being excused for the sick and twisted things they do. At least half of the misogynistic comments that you sent are from women. Rape culture is based on mind control, teaching girls and women to silence and attack women who speak out on behalf of women and to also defend male abusers.

For any person, however, male or female, who has the intellectual power to decode the messages of rape culture, the "reward" isn't gender-specific at all. It's blacklisting and erasure. There is little difference between men and women when it comes to speaking truth. You become a target for Nazis. Truth is the enemy of rape culture and patriarchy. Truth destroys lies, so it's quite dangerous to liars.

**JD: What is your advice to someone who strongly believes in something but takes a lot of heat for being outspoken about it?**

RB: Make sure it is based on fact, data, and scientific proof instead of belief systems that cannot be proven.

**JD: Thank you so much for taking the time to do this interview. And, again, thank you for standing up and speaking out when you feel that you should.**

*@Whitney Gage*

I'm hoping that maybe, somehow, my story can help someone else. If it's just one person, I'm perfectly okay with that. When I was eighteen, my parents had just divorced and my boyfriend of three years broke up with me. I couldn't afford the college I had worked so hard to get into, and I was very naïve. I took a semester off to figure out what to do next. I bounced from house to house, wasting time with people who didn't really deserve it.

I partied a lot. I didn't do any drugs, but I liked to drink because it helped me to temporarily forget about the things I was going through. A friend of mine invited me to a party with people I knew and trusted in my hometown. There was only one person at the party who I didn't know. He was seemingly pleasant, we had mutual friends, and he greeted me when I walked in.

My friend and I had planned to spend the night so that we didn't have to drive. We were going to sleep overnight in one of the rooms in the house. While she was playing a drinking game, I decided that I was tired of partying. My ex-boyfriend (who I had remained friends with) took me to the room where I was going to sleep and covered me with a blanket. I hadn't eaten all day, and he knew I'd get sick if I didn't. He went to get some food for me. While he was gone, I fell asleep. I may have passed out. I'm not sure which it was.

I don't know how long it had been when I woke up. When I opened my eyes, I saw my friend on the bed to the right of me, having sex with a guy friend of ours. The one person I didn't know at the party, the guy who had greeted me when I walked in, was on top of me. I was naked pinned under him, and my head was pounding. My leg was numb and it took me a moment to realize it was because he was digging his knee into my thigh to keep me from moving. I tried to push him off, but I couldn't. I grabbed my phone to call my ex-boyfriend, but the guy on top of me threw it across the room. The people on the bed next to me might as well have been nonexistent through the entire thing. My throat felt tight. I couldn't scream. It was like one of those dreams where your feet are glued to the ground, and you can't run. My vocal cords must have been held by those same grips.

After what seemed like a very long time, my ex-boyfriend burst in the door. Seeing him somehow gave me the strength to push the guy off, but not before he caused bruises and cuts on my arms and legs. My ex-boyfriend grabbed me, rushing me to his truck and, despite my pleading, ran back inside to try to find the guy who had already run to his car and left.

My ex-boyfriend took me to the police station. We gave statements. I was rushed to the hospital for a rape kit. I didn't know how to react. They gave me medication that made me vomit. I felt so broken. I called my mom, whose sobs only brought more of my own. The same thing had happened to her at age 15, and I hadn't remembered that until I made the call. Both of our hearts were broken.

I pressed charges. The district attorney was an old mentor of mine, one of the perks of being from a small town, I guess. He fought on my behalf, but the statements from people who were at the party were not in my favor. My "friends" were afraid that their parents would find out what they had been doing that night. A few of them admitted that to me, as if it were an acceptable reason for why they wouldn't help me try to find some peace.

The jury, naturally, found my "drunken state" to be my own fault. The rape kit did show forced penetration, but that didn't seem to matter because I had been drunk. "Maybe you didn't want your ex-boyfriend to know you wanted sex with that person, so you made this all up," someone said to me. They said that the clothes I had been wearing that night were suggestive. I had been wearing a simple black t-shirt and a pair of denim shorts.

I lost my case. The guy who raped me moved to Arkansas the following week. People who I had called "friends" said that I was too dramatic to be in their lives. They had no concern for my feelings, no concern about the fact that I couldn't wear jeans for a month, and no concern that I cried every single day in the shower so that my mom wouldn't find me crying in bed. I developed anxiety that I struggle with to this day. I don't like crowds, and I am always uncomfortable around male strangers.

The only place I find hope is in the fact that I have a very loving family and a very small circle of dear friends. There was no grand lesson in what happened to me, nor did it bring me any closure. But, I know now that I can find strength in helping others. It's all I want to do in life. I fight every day to remind myself that I am worth more than what those awful people told me I was. I am strong, independent, intelligent, and always armed. But most importantly, I am confident. My value is not in what I lost that night, but in what I live my life for now. I strive to share my message and Vine is my means of doing so. If I can share my story, perhaps someone on Vine will find comfort and reassurance that they're not alone.

# @Caitlin Noel

When I was fifteen, I was hanging out with a person I thought I could trust. He was a bit older, and he had never given me the impression that he could be harmful or untrustworthy. He had also never shown any romantic interest toward me. I thought of him as a friend. One day, when I was alone, he asked if he could stop over to see me. He was acting strangely, but I didn't think much of it.

I fell asleep watching a movie and I woke up to him touching me inappropriately. I was scared and wasn't sure how to respond. I didn't want to anger him. He seemed really aggravated and powerful. I told him that I did not want to participate in what he was doing. In response, he smacked me. I began to cry, and he smacked me again.

I didn't know what to do. No one was home. He went too far. Any time I tried to object, he smacked me harder. He finished, and then he left without a word. I hate myself to this day for what happened, though I don't know what I could have done to change it. The worst part was that for months, I felt as if I had to hang out with our mutual group of friends and act as if nothing was wrong. I didn't want to tell anyone.

I'm twenty-two now. I recently told my mom about it. She was raped in college, and she had never told anyone about her experience. She is already on board at the shelter in our city, and I will start volunteering. Jessi Smiles, Jen Dent, and so many others on Vine have truly helped me deal with something I've been going through for seven years.

I can't tell you how truly thankful I am for that.

## *Anonymous Viner*

Over the course of two years, beginning when I was nine years old, my babysitter's teenage son sexually assaulted me. I knew that it felt wrong, but I didn't know why. I didn't know what I should do about it. I was afraid that my babysitter would get mad at me. When I was 13 years old, I told my dad about it. I begged him not to say anything, but he went and spoke with my offender's dad, who then beat his son physically.

I lost my innocence in a traumatic way. During the years that the assault was happening, I prayed to God every day and night that something bad would happen to my babysitter's son. I prayed that a school bus would hit him. I prayed that he would get cancer. I prayed for him to die in gruesome ways. Being so young and dealing with this on my own led me to question the validity of God and, frankly, any good in the world at all.

When I was around 14 years old, I found out that my babysitter's son actually did have cancer. I had finally gotten around to coping with my abuse the best way I knew how. I had a boyfriend and had somewhat "forgotten" about what had happened to me. When I found out that my babysitter's son had cancer, I blamed myself. I felt that God had finally answered my prayers and in turn, the cancer was my fault. I felt terribly guilty.

While hospitalized, my babysitter's son woke up from a drugged sleep, screaming, "Tell her I'm sorry!" Later, when he was awake and alert, his father asked him what he meant. He told his father that he was talking about me. He said that he wanted a conversation with me and to apologize. His father came to me with the request. I declined. In my own mind, I had decided to forgive him, but what happened to me changed my life forever and I will never forget the terrible things he did. I will never be able to shake the feeling that all people can do terrible things. He skewed my vision of the world and the people in it. I will never give him the gratification of feeling as though I accept his apology or that I am okay with what happened.

I have always used potentially offensive, sexual humor as a coping mechanism. I do that to hide the fact that I am over sensitive about my sexuality. I began to vine for fun and to make my friends laugh, but I quickly met some amazing, inspirational, and wonderful people, and Jessi Smiles is one of them. I'm proud of her for standing up for herself, and for not responding to the victim-blaming and slut-shaming antics of people on Vine. She rose above all that with class and grace.

My experience allows me to feel empathy for victims and to also pity the attacker. A person who hurts another person so deeply must be going through terrible issues in his or her own life. I hope and pray that the people who hurt others can get the help that they need to change. I also understand that most of those people are stuck in a vortex of denial and will never admit fault, much less seek help. Vine was originally intended to be an outlet for me to express myself, but it has become much more than that. I really needed this.

Jen,

In October of 2013, after watching your vines and seeing your determination to fight for your friends, I was faced with old feelings of pain cause by memories that I had shut out. I was molested by two different family members from the ages of seven to eleven years old. I blocked those feelings after my mom yelled at me for talking about my abuse. She wanted me to keep it a secret. The same thing had happened to her as a child. Since she had never told anyone about her abuse, she thought I should do the same.

My abuse began in church during service. I was sitting with a boy. I remember feeling bad and thinking that I was going to Hell. It amazes me that I still loved to go to church after that.

It took me a while to tell my mom. She talked to the boy's mom about it. His mother blamed me, saying that I was an overaffectionate child. Because of that, I have always questioned myself, wondering if it was my fault.

A few years later, my family moved to Arizona. I tried to make myself stop thinking about it, and tried to live as a normal child. All that changed when my brother became friends with a new boy who my family trusted. One day, he wanted me to play a "game" with him. I felt bad and evil for doing what he asked of me, and I told him so. He threatened to kill my mom if I said anything about it.

I didn't tell anyone because I was scared. This little "game" of his continued for a few more years. When I finally said something to my mother, his true, evil nature came to light. It turned out that he was also molesting his niece and was creating pornography from it. He was fifteen when this all started. I am so glad that I found the strength to say something when I finally did.

I have never really spoken about these things because my mother told me not to, but because of you and your vines I am not afraid anymore. I am allowing myself to heal. In turn, I want to help others who are like me. My hope is that I can help people understand that they don't have to keep secrets like I did.

Without Vine, I don't feel that I would have had such a great opportunity to reach out to people.

I was the avid "wild child" in a happy, stable home with a mom, dad, and older brother. We weren't rich, but we were comfortable, and happy. While my family planned for most things, there was one thing that none of us could have planned for or even imagined. It was the loss of innocence of their only daughter. I was five years old when my life was forever damaged at the hands of my babysitter and her boyfriend. It comes to me now in pieces and flashes of fragmented memories. A smell, a look, a feeling. That's all I have of it now. My life before has been forgotten. It is gone, wiped from existence. It is as though I had died and was reborn as someone of whom I was unprepared to face. It is the aftermath that proved to be more scarring.

My family was one of internalization, and my sexual abuse was never dealt with head on. My father moved to America at the age of seventeen. He grew up in Greece where rules were stricter, punishments were harsher, and emotions were put aside. He didn't have the room in his soul to deal with what happened. The only way he knew how to cope was by using misdirected anger. As I child, I saw my family crack to the core without a bandage and this led me to convince myself, at my tender age, that I was the one to blame.

From then on, my life was a stream of self-punishment. I felt as if I were branded with a giant "abuse victim" marking on my forehead and that everyone who saw me knew that I was unclean and broken. My adolescent life was spent jumping from one mutilation to the next and from one addiction to the next. I didn't know how to handle romantic relationships. I was on a train headed for a brick wall. I use to hide in small spaces in my house and rip at my skin. One day, I slashed my forearm so badly that I couldn't hide it from my mother. She cornered me in the kitchen as I cried. My poor mother had to deal with my wild outbursts, my unpredictable behavior, and my constant craziness. I had finally broken her too, another victim of my wasted life.

Although I was lonely, I was never alone. I surrounded myself with lots of friends. I was the funny, crazy, wild girl. I was anything they wanted me to be because I was terrified of being known as the broken girl. Once people know your truth, they will never look at you the same way. This persona followed me to college, accompanied with a mix of heavy drugs, alcohol and sexual promiscuity. I would do anything people asked of me because I had no self worth. I meant so little to myself that I would gladly drink a bottle of vodka and jump out of a window. Who would care if I died? I certainly didn't.

I was in a relationship with someone who told me how amazing I was one day only to turn around and tell me the next day that if I didn't get on my knees that I was as good as dead. I felt dead. It wasn't until I was sitting on my dorm room floor with a bottle of pills spread out in front of me, that I was finally forced to face myself. I don't know why I didn't die that day. It's not as if I cared, to be honest. I dropped out of college a few weeks later. I went back to my hometown, got a nothing job, and lived a meaningless life. Then, I met my husband.

He appeared from out of nowhere at a time in my life when I felt like a feather on the line of life and death that could blow either way. He saved me. He loved me. Scars, baggage, and all. He was the first person who I ever told my story to and the first person I trusted enough to not break under the weight of my secret. That was the last thing I wanted: To break someone else. I had already broken my family.

He was strong. He encouraged me to be the wild and funny girl, but he also taught me that it was okay to be broken. I needed to know that it was acceptable to fall apart because there was someone who would help me put the pieces back together.

Here I am 12 years later, facing every anxiety that has ever held me back in the form of a front facing camera and a six-second timeline. My first vine was a clip of a documentary that I was watching. No one liked it and I didn't gain any followers from it, but I honestly didn't care. I found myself growing in the Vine world and reaching out. I have engaged with some of the most amazing people, and I have formed some real, true friendships that I will be eternally grateful for. I have had the opportunity to speak my mind, as well as to speak out and speak up without fear of judgment.

Whenever I'm having a rough moment, I get on Vine and talk about the most ridiculous things I can come up with. I have learned to use my humor as a form of expression and release as opposed to the mask to which I had become accustomed. I still carry my pain, and I do struggle with it from time to time, but is great to have a community of friends to call on when I need them.

I'm KateRex the Viner but, more important, I'm Kate the human.

## Anonymous Viner

Hi Jen,

I have been meaning to write you this email for the past few weeks. I regret not saying these things to you earlier, but I feel it is past time.

When things came to a head with the Jessi situation, it was impossible to not notice what was going on online. As a victim of sexual assault and molestation myself, I was so deeply affected by what was going on.

I experienced a minor emotional breakdown because I felt so completely triggered by the things that people were saying to you and Jessi. I was in so much pain, but completely unable to say anything myself. I felt so broken and I was afraid to have anyone attack me. I would not have been able to take it. I really contemplated disappearing off Vine and other social media. For the first time in years, I was having flashbacks. I was paranoid, anxious, scared, and ANGRY.

I kept watching, and I saw you and Jessi NOT break. I watched you two become even stronger despite the constant vitriol spewed at you. You got through and OWNED the situation. The best part is that I got better. I started standing up for my feelings.

I wanted you to know that I am sincerely sorry that I didn't have the guts to go public with my feelings, but I did learn to stick up for myself. If ever you wondered if you empowered even ONE woman, you empowered me.

I'm a stay at home mom of two small children (my older son has autism). I have been using the app myself as a way to get myself out of the house and find beauty in being a mother/homemaker/blogger. I've connected with so many other parents who have taught me to find beauty in the every day. I make vines with my children and have seen my older son's imagination finally blossom, as he thinks of vines we can make together. I involve him in all my vines, and it has strengthened our bond so much.

Thank you so much for helping me appreciate what it is to be a WOMAN.

I love you.

# @Morning Wood

I met the man of my dreams on a sultry day in New Orleans. Little did I know then that the man of my dreams would soon become the monster of my nightmares. I wasn't supposed to be in New Orleans that day, but as fate would have it, I was off work and had a pocket full of money. I thought "What the hell?" I loaded up my car and headed for the Big Easy with a party on my mind. As soon as I left the hotel, I passed my ideal man walking down the street. He had a shaved head, tattoos, and piercings. As we passed each other, we made eye contact. I looked back and saw him jogging back toward me.

"Can I take you to dinner?" he asked, and just like that we were a couple. After only a couple of months, he asked me to move in. At first, our life was like a fairytale. He was twenty-four years my senior, and a man of means. He had his own house, car, and business. With me, now he had his trophy "wife." We ruled the night. The booze flowed like water, the lights showed brighter, and the music never stopped. Just as quickly, however, the honeymoon phase ended.

I had heard stories about him since the beginning of our relationship, but I always chalked those stories up to petty jealousies and catty banter, both of which were commonplace in New Orleans' gay culture. He had voluntarily told me about suicide attempts and short stays in mental institutions over love that he had lost. I swept those stories under the rug as things of the past that were no longer important.

After two years of living together, I noticed that the attention he lavished on me was beginning to feel restrictive, but he remained so charming that I was convinced there was nothing malicious about it. It wasn't until a joint birthday party we threw for ourselves that I saw how crazy he could actually be.

We invited all of our friends and family. We threw a huge party. It was a great night until we got into an argument. It was a petty fight over jealousies that were spawned by rumors. He took me into a room and wouldn't let me out. My aunt tried to come in, and he pushed her to the ground, kicking her in the ribs. I had never seen this side of him before. He looked like a demon. My aunt and I ran from the house as he chased us, waving a knife in the air.

We were separated for a month while I slept on a friend's couch. Slowly, but surely, he won me back with apologies and promises. I gave in and moved back in with him. I got a great paying job in the film industry. Life seemed even better than before. We worked hard and partied harder.

My work hours were crazy. I worked 16-hour days and, the whole time I was working, he would drink at the bar. He would call me at work, drunkenly slurring and accusing me of being out "fucking around" on him. He constantly called my friends and coworkers, spouting all kinds of venom. Sometimes he made 30 phone calls a night while I was at work. Some nights, I couldn't concentrate on my job responsibilities out of fear of what would happen when I got home.

The next time we had a huge fight, my mother was there. He held a pair of scissors to my throat, threatening to take my life. Even after he did that in front of my mother, I stayed and listened to a month of apologies and promises. That time, he even promised to get therapy.

I quit my job in the film industry because the hours were "too much for our relationship to handle". I began working for him. We were together around the clock, at home and at work. He did not pay me. All the money we made at work went into his account, and he paid all the bills, which were in his name. My phone, my car, and the house were all in his name. Everything belonged to him.

His behavior became increasingly controlling. He listened at the door when I was in the bathroom. He followed me when I left the house. He even had people watching me. He demanded the passwords to my all my accounts. We began to lose our friends, and my family wouldn't visit me because the stress that surrounded us was palpable. Soon, he had me exactly me where he wanted me: All to himself.

One night, I awoke as he was punching me in the face. Everything was a bloody blur. His eyes were crazed, as though something had taken over him. As I fought my way out from under him and jumped out of bed, he drew a knife and began to chase me around the house. As I grabbed my cell phone and ran out the door, he lunged toward me, tearing off my shirt. It was three o'clock in the morning. I ran down the streets of New Orleans, bloody, in nothing but my boxer shorts and socks.

I decided that I would never go back to him. It has not been an easy road. His emotional warfare continues to this day with his never-ending, venom-filled voicemails and emails. There are days where he sits in his vehicle on the street outside my house. There are days where I feel as though I can't breathe, and I feel like a prisoner in my own home.
There are times where I don't think I will ever get through this. Vine saved my life. The community I found on this simple app has changed my life. I was at the end of my rope and about to slip off, but I have been pulled back up in six-seconds intervals. I have made great friends that I know I can count on, and they can count on me.

## @Kenzie Kath

I joined Vine when it first started back in January of 2013. I started doing the typical vines that everyone else does, progressing into impressions and talking about life. I started following Jen Dent because I thought she was hilarious. When she began posting more vines about standing up for people who couldn't speak for themselves, she empowered me; she has truly been my Vine superhero.

When the Jessi Smiles incident happened, I didn't know how to react, but when I saw that there were tons of other people on Vine who felt the same way as I did, I felt inspired. I was a little discouraged when I saw all the hate. I had dealt with some bullying in the past with a couple vines I had done, but nothing like this.

Young kids believed the lies and were calling people extremely disrespectful names. It was very disappointing to see how these kids who really have no life experience yet, seemed to believe that someone who is "good looking" or "funny" isn't capable of raping someone. I had also noticed this type of behavior when the Duck Dynasty, Phil Robertson issue took place, where he had made homophobic remarks in an interview with GQ magazine. People, especially young kids, were very angry with the gay community for speaking out about what they believed Phil Robertson had done wrong. I, myself, posted a vine about it and received death threats and insults.

Before those two incidents, I had never encountered people who were so willing to be mean to someone they had never met. I've been called plenty of names on Vine and other social media outlets, including "fat", "ugly" and my favorite "fat, ugly, lesbian". That one cracks me up every single time. How does one look like a lesbian? And what is so wrong with that?

I try to use Vine in a positive way. Bullying doesn't get to me, but I know that many young people feel as though it's the end of the world when they are bullied. My sister is a teenager, and she has tried to take her own life a handful of times because of what people have said to her. What's sad is that she is a very talented and beautiful young woman with a lot of potential. She doesn't have the experience or understanding that life goes on. You have to forget about words that are spoken to you. You have to rise above them. I've suffered from depression and anxiety for as long as I can remember, and Vine has been a place where I can meet others with the same issues. It's also a place where I can see the positivity people are putting out into the world. My hope is that kids will realize that the words bullies say to them don't matter. I would also like those bullies to know that while words may be temporary, the damage they can do is real and can cause lifelong pain to others.

# Nine

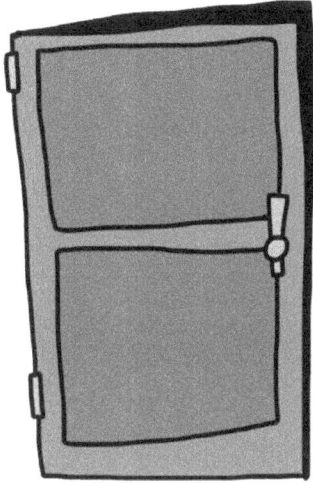

## *Vine Comes Out*

## @Kate G

I've known that I was gay for years, and it is a major part of my life, but I needed to eventually come out to my parents. Never would I have imagined that Vine would play a major role in that process.

I downloaded Vine in March of 2013. I vined random things that I found interesting, and I thought it was cool because I'm a film major and aspire to be a cinematographer. I love anything that involves a camera. Vine was a natural attraction.

I met @Mady D. during Vine Prom, a fun and silly event Viners created where we all pretended we were celebrating at a dance party. We hit it off and became friends. In December, I received some devastating news, and needed a distraction. I got on Vine. That night, Mady and I made vines for each other wearing paper mustaches and singing. To the outside world, that night may seem meaningless and silly, but to me, that night helped me cope with something that I had never dealt with before. Mady helped me in many ways that night. She helped me forget my problems, even if only for a few hours.

A few weeks later, Mady asked if I would like to get on Oovoo. It was 2am my time, but I decided to do it. It was the first time that she and I talked for longer than six seconds. Before I knew it, it was 6:30 in the morning. The connection between the two of us is something I can't even begin to put into words. We are similar in so many ways.

I also met @Emmanuel the Llama on Vine. We talked on Oovoo and became close friends. He is an outgoing, crazy character, and that is what I love most about him. He is genuine in everything he does.

On Sunday March 9th, 2014, I woke up knowing that this was the day that I would come out to my parents. I sent Mady a text and told her how scared I was. She asked whether I would mind if she made a vine wishing me luck, and I told her she could. After she made hers, Emmanuel made one and used the hash tag #AdviceForKate. Instantly, I began to receive likes, comments, and follows from people that I had never met. It was overwhelming because I had never received that much love from strangers before. I decided to vine the process of coming out to my family. The hash tag exploded. I was getting so many responses that I couldn't keep up with them all. All day, I was on the verge of tears because of all the support I was getting from Vine.

On Vine, there is always some sort of drama going on. That day, I did not see any drama. I did not receive a single hate comment throughout day, which is almost unheard-of. Everyone was supportive and positive. When I came out to my parents, I wasn't that afraid. The love from Vine relaxed me and turned my fear into excitement. My parents took the news very well, just as everyone told me they would. They still love me, no matter what, and will always support me through thick and thin.

I'm no different from anyone else. I'm just a kid who has been helped by Vine many times. I know that there are people who have gone through much harder times than I, and are not as blessed to have the support that I had that day. I'm proud that some people view me as an inspiration. People tell me that I have helped them accept themselves as who they are. People have shared so many coming out stories with me. The fact that my story affected so many people brings me to tears. I love that I can help people be okay with who they are.

I would never have believed that my life would change so much because of Vine.

# @Mady D.

The hash tag #AdviceForKate was created for a friend who was in
need of support, and the people on Vine totally stepped up. I met
Kate G. through Vine a few months ago, and our friendship was
almost immediate. It's strange to see someone only in 6-second
increments and to feel as though you are connected to them. I could
tell that Kate was a beautiful soul and from the first time we chatted
outside of Vine, I found that to be true.

Kate told me about her plans to come out to her parents. Coming out
is a major event in someone's life, and to share it with her viewers
would be a beautiful thing. She said that there was a possibility that
her parents already knew, but she wasn't sure. She was nervous.
Who wouldn't be? I did my best to comfort and reassure her, but I
had never been in her shoes. My coming out story wasn't as stressful
as Kate's. My grandmother, aunt, and big brother are all gay, so
when I told my family, the shock turned instantly into love.

I had never felt the pressure of possibly being disowned by my own
parents. Once I ran out of my own words of encouragement for Kate,
I turned to Vine. I wished her luck and asked my followers to do the

same. I came up with the hash tag in hopes that her story would reach more people. @Emmanuel the Llama pitched in, and together we got #AdviceForKate trending for most of the day. It was insane! People came out of nowhere to wish Kate good luck and to offer her advice.

I turned to Vine because it is full of people who are capable of doing and saying good things. When directed to the right cause, Vine is magical and healing. I knew that there had to be several thousand members of the LGBT community on Vine, and I knew that they, along with their supporters, would love to share their stories and offer Kate the type of encouragement that she needed.

Vine constantly reaffirms my faith in humans. People are inherently meant to be good. The ones who are negative just haven't felt what it is like to be good yet. On that day, #AdviceForKate allowed many people to see what it is like to not only *be* good but to *do* good. Vine is a character builder and emotional healer. It provides comic relief. It's a trendy place to hang out with friends.

Kate will forever remember the day she came out to her parents, and not just because she vined it. She will remember it because, for 6 seconds at a time, her life and the lives of people watching and participating were connected in ways they had never been before.

## @Emmanuel The Llama

When I first downloaded Vine, I was going through so much. I had been experiencing harassment at work for being gay. I ended up being homeless for a short time. I knew what it was like to be an outcast, to feel unwanted and worthless. I thought that if I brought some positivity to other peoples' lives, making them laugh and smile, it would make me happy in turn. Sometimes I did characters. Other times, I simply reminded people that, even in the darkest places, there is light in the world.

I spent most of my early days on Vine viewing other peoples' videos and laughing. I began to see people asking for guidance and support. Some of the heavier subject matter I noticed people vining about involved gay rights, self-image, and depression. I thought, "In these six seconds, maybe I can help someone."

I didn't realize that my vines would affect people so positively. I began to receive so many comments and emails from people who thanked me for supporting them. They told me that just hearing that they were not alone helped them in ways I couldn't understand. I would read those messages and cry, and sometimes I would laugh. I was at the lowest point in my life, yet I was helping other people. When I helped Kate G. on the day that she came out to her parents, I was filled with emotion. So many good-hearted people came out to help with that hash tag.

I use Vine to show my love and support, not only for the LGBT community but also for anyone who needs it. I make people smile. I share my life with people. Those of us who interact on this little app are a family. I care very deeply for those people. That's a powerful thing.

# @*Cadyn Rocket*

If you had told me a year ago that a social media app would change my life, I wouldn't believe you. I was a senior in high school dealing with the drama of college applications, SATs, and graduation. I didn't have the hardest life. I wasn't living on the streets or starving. I was simply a boy trapped inside the body of a female.

I come from a family of Bible thumping, closed minded people. They are one picket sign away from being members of Westboro Baptist Church. I had a very difficult time growing up. I have known from the age of four that I **hated** being a girl. Every aspect of being a female completely grossed me out. My parents were in complete denial and refused to help me in any way. They insisted that I was trying to find a way to disappoint them and defy God. They automatically assumed that I was a lesbian. For a while, I let them believe that lie. Adapting to that stereotype was easier than saying, "I am a male but I have a vagina." For years, I lied to everyone. In the back of my mind, I knew that I was not a lesbian.

Looking for a way to escape from the real world, I downloaded Vine. Many of my friends were talking about it, so why not? I set up a profile and regretfully chose the screen name "Taylor Rocket." Taylor Rocket was a persona that I adopted in high school to make my name less girly. I created my Vine profile and started posting stupid six-second videos.

As time passed, I became more involved with Vine. I came across some inspirational people like Tobie Stevens and Jen Dent. There were so many people putting themselves out there without caring about what anyone thought. Watching this, I began to consider coming out. I didn't want to be Taylor Rocket anymore. I didn't want to lie any longer. I wanted to stop being offended when people listed me as their "Woman Crush Wednesday." I didn't want to continue hiding the biggest part my life from everyone. I called my best friend, who I met on Vine. His name is Trent Asher Allen.

Slowly, I gained the courage to change my name to Cadyn. I told my story in pieces. I began to see a community of people who accepted and adored me. No one cared about the fact that I was born a woman. Everyone simply wanted to know more about what I was going through at that point in my life. I had never had so much unconditional support in my life. Vine changed my whole world. I never thought I could be my real self until I found Vine.

*Ten*

*Cheerleaders, Activists, and Advocates*

# @Crunk Panda™

I've always looked after others, even when it has proven to be detrimental to me. It's encoded in my DNA. I was raised in a police family, and I served active duty Air Force for 17 years. Standing up and speaking out is just like breathing to me. When I see someone down, I want to help them stand. When I see someone crying I want to make them smile. When I see things that I view as horribly wrong, I want to make them stop. I want to expose those things.

I'm not always right, but luckily for me I've been more right than wrong.

I've always possessed a certain leadership quality. It began in childhood and grew stronger during my military career. People have always looked to me for help. Vine allows me to contribute, not only to others but also to myself. Vine and its users are like therapy for me. I suffer from anxiety, and have some issues that are directly connected to the time I spent in military service, which was ultimately the reason that I am no longer active in the Air Force.

I choose to use what I've seen, heard, and experienced in my life to empower other people around me, and to show them that they are not alone. There are so many young people on Vine, and I feel somewhat of a responsibility to try and mentor them when I can. I can offer them a unique perspective.

I've reached out to several kids and talked to them outside Vine. I'm not *their* parent, but I am a parent, and I try to help them by offering a different point of view. I'm not one to judge, and I'm not a saint by any stretch of the imagination. I often tell others that the good I do today is because I became cognizant of past behaviors. Now, I am trying to atone for those things.

Sometimes people just need to talk and vent. I've been there myself, many times. Venting to someone you don't know can be almost therapeutic. You don't always feel as though you can talk to people who see you every day. Sometimes, you need someone who cares because they choose to, not because they are related to you or have known you for a long time. I want to be that person who listens for as many people as I can. I want to be that shoulder to lean on.

I don't sympathize; I empathize. Vine users help me more than they will ever know.
Not every day is a good day, but not every day has to be a bad day. There are times when I hear my text notification, see a name, and immediately know that the message can't be anything good. It hurts to put myself out there sometimes, especially for those who really do look for guidance, but I'm going to keep doing it.

I always tell people that I am as nice as they will let me be. I try to live that way. I know my outward appearance and words may seem to contradict actions, but don't let looks fool you. I've found angels in the oddest of places.

# @*Antoine Felonius Tate*

*Antoine Felonius Tate is best known for creating the Black Vine Entertainment Awards (BVEAs) that ran on Vine in December 2013. The awards developed a cult following with rave reviews. It has since been turned into a full-length video and can be found on PoppinMedia.com.*

A year ago, I worked as an intern for the Pennsylvania House of Representatives. I had convinced myself that I was destined to thrive in a political career; however, my heart wasn't in it. I like politics; however, I love art, film, and music. I moved to Los Angeles after I received an internship offer from a production company.

I consider myself to be a "social medialist." Yes, I made that word up. I coined that phrase because I use almost every popular social media app that is available. Every few minutes, I check my Facebook, Twitter, Vine, Instagram, and Kik. At least once a day, I check my YouTube, Tumblr, LinkedIn, Pinterest, Ok Hello, and WhatsApp. Occasionally, I check my Pheed and Myspace. Yes, Myspace!

Prior to Vine, I was doing YouTube videos. I posted videos of my own fashion shows, plays, films, and various other projects that I had created. I frequently checked the App Store to see what the most popular new apps were. One day as I was browsing I discovered Vine.

When I originally started vining, I used it like everyone else. My first vine was a video of random things in my room. Soon, I began documenting my life at work, school, and home. I had only a few followers, but I didn't care. Initially, my home feed was filled with real-life friends. It took me a while to figure out that there was a huge community on the app, and the introduction of the revine button changed everything.

We all thought that Vine would fade away in favor of Instagram, but the revine button saved it. Because of that button, I saw many different genres of vines on my home feed. As a result, I started getting more involved. I began tagging popular Viners, participating in hash tags and in return, I started to gain some recognition. The more I networked, the more friends I made. I went from having Vine acquaintances to developing real friendships. Now, I talk to a few of my friends from Vine almost every day though I still haven't met them in person.

Vine kept me sane when I arrived in LA. I had a few friends, but I barely saw them due to the distance. To entertain myself, I watched vines. I quickly learned that it was more than an app. It became a way of life for me. I found myself living in this virtual world for at least a few hours every day. Once I learned the power of Vine, I decided that my niche would be to inspire and entertain people through my creativity.

*On the BVEAs:*

I realized that far too many talented people on Vine were unnoticed. Many Viners do not receive their deserved recognition because they are not on the Popular Now page. One day, I saw a Viner named @Flizzle create a hash tag asking Viners to vote on who should win in certain Vine categories. I thought it was an interesting idea that could work on a much bigger scale.

Initially, the BVEAs were going to be a fun parody of the BET Awards for my close circle of friends, but as the idea snowballed and gained more attention I realized that this event had the potential to be a movement for Vine. The awards were not intended just for a specific race, though the title indicated otherwise. I chose to keep the original title as I wanted to stay true to the group of people who initially supported it.

The awards changed my entire perspective of Vine. I quickly realized that I could greatly benefit from the app. I could gain followers, gain media attention, get paid, and more. My follower count skyrocketed on all my social media accounts, and I was catapulted into a new world of Vine. While I do not have as many followers as some of the popular Viners, I can get in contact with many of them because of the recognition I gained through the awards. I can honestly go anywhere in the country and connect with people from Vine whether it is for social or business reasons.

People were entertained, inspired, and amazed with the BVEAs. I received emails, texts, messages, and phone calls from people telling me how proud they were. In addition, many people who were featured on the awards received a boost in followers. They gained the recognition that they deserved. That night, people learned that Vine was more than a social media app.

*On December 30, a random group of Vine friends and acquaintances held the 2013 Vine Awards. That award show was put together very quickly. It was simply for fun and was not planned or structured in any way. The people involved were unaware that the BVEAs had taken place. Soon, the 2013 Vine Awards account began to receive thousands of angry comments and accusations of stealing the idea from the BVEAs.*

The BVEAs were very popular. Many Viners spoke out against the event, claiming that it was exclusive only to African-Americans. This sparked a huge war on Vine, and my supporters fought on my behalf. The supporters were ready to attack anyone who disrespected the awards show.

The day after the BVEAs, some of my followers discovered that someone was having the 2013 Vine Awards. This sparked a whole new outrage as people were convinced that the other awards show was copying the BVEAs. From lack of knowledge, I assumed the same thing. First, I was angry, but I decided to research the event and I quickly learned that the 2013 Vine Awards were completely different. I found myself laughing hysterically at the vines on that account. Before my followers had a chance to start posting negative comments on the awards posts, I posted a vine showing my support and spent the evening revining them. I suppose I helped calm a storm before it fully began.

Vine has helped me mentally, socially, and professionally. Through Vine, I can support thousands of people. Ironically, the night that I was doing the BVEAs I was terrified. I thought the show was going horribly because it took hours to finish, but I was overwhelmed by the responses. There was some negativity, but the positivity outweighed the negativity by a landslide. Because of that, I know that I will receive support despite what venture I undertake next.

## @*Tobie Stevens*

For as long as I can remember, I've been full of energy and possessed an overwhelming amount of love and joy. All I have ever wanted to do was to share that with other people. Vine is a place where I can. I began vining in May 2013, never expecting that it would completely change my life.

When I first got on Vine, I goofed around and watched other people's vines. One night, I happened upon the Late Night Party Patrol (@LNPP). They welcomed me with open arms, and I am now lucky to call them my friends.

My follower count rose faster than I could have ever anticipated. It surprised me because I use my Vine as more of a vlog than anything else. I am known for over-posting. That has never seemed to bother my followers, or as I call them, my "Wildflowers". They love all my posts, no matter what kind they are.

I love to do inspirational vines most of all. Those vines are my pride and joy. I want to make people feel as though they are enough. I want them to know that they are important and that people care about them. Vine opened a huge door for me in allowing me to do these things daily.

I'm very open with my followers and in turn, they are always there for me. They write the most heartwarming letters to me, in which they tell me their own struggles and how I have helped them become stronger. They tell me how their faith has been renewed or how their outlook on Christianity has changed because of how open I am about my relationship with Christ.

Thanks to Vine, I have been awarded the privilege of speaking at middle schools across the state of South Carolina. I speak with students concerning self-image and the negative effects of bullying. I also recently spoke at a youth conference about my walk with Christ and how social media affects it. Vine is almost a type of therapy for me.

It's been an amazing journey. I have received much negativity and hatred, but I'm getting better at not letting it bother me. For every negative comment I get, I get at least 20 letters from my Wildflowers telling me that my vines helped them stop cutting, to seek help, or to simply believe in themselves. That is why I vine.

## @Jen Dent

I've lived in the same small town my whole life. I've always loved to act. I have videos of myself putting on skits from very early on in my life. I've always had an innate need to be creative and to express myself. Most of the people I know in real life have always told me that I'm funny, though I don't have many friends who share the same interests.

I've been on social media for as long as it has been available. I began on dial-up internet going into chat rooms. I have friends from online who I've never met in real life; however, we have been friends for almost 20 years. A girl that I met online and have never seen face-to-face decided what word I would tattoo on my wrist three years ago: "True".

Social media sites like Facebook and YouTube are great, but when I found out about Vine, it was perfect. It's a way to interact with creative people who enjoy expressing themselves. On Facebook, my followers always wondered why I was so random and open. On Vine, most people are like me in that respect.

I believe Vine has helped with my stress. One of my first popular vines was when I was driving around, visiting patients. It was the middle of summer, and I was wearing uncomfortable pants. I made a spur of the moment vine and complained about "my fucking pants!"

There was such a huge response to that vine. I wasn't expecting it, and it felt good to know that people identified with such a silly little problem. It's easy to think you're the only one with those issues. It turns out; many people hate their fucking pants.

Some Viners do a lot of planning and post once a day or even less. There are some amazing vines out there from those people. I'm in awe quite often, left with my jaw hanging open from what I just witnessed. That's not how I vine. If I have an idea, I do it. I've tried waiting to post things, but it just drives me crazy until I post them. I guess it's the gift and curse of having a very active imagination. I can't hold onto an idea. I have to get it out.

I'm not afraid to vine about my life, and I'm not afraid to stand up for things I believe in. I don't do things just so certain people will follow me. I've lost tons of followers because I post what I want, as much as I want, and as often as I want. I've also lost followers because I speak up about things, and I'm loud when I do it.

For a while, losing followers bothered me. I saw losing followers as a negative thing. Then I realized that more people stick around than those who leave. I interact regularly with my followers. I have many amazing friends who I met on Vine. I talk to those friends more than I talk to my real-life friends, which might seem like a bad thing, but it's just the way it is. People from Vine have really helped me through some tough times.

I often get messages telling me how much of a difference I have made in people's lives. Even after almost a year of this, I am still dumbfounded when they tell me how much I matter to them. When I get negativity from others, I just try to think about the people who care about me. I try to think about the people who have thanked me for just being myself.

You can't please everyone. I know I'm not perfect. I have my bad parts just like everyone else, but everything I do is coming from a place of love for someone somewhere. It's a learning process. I can't make everyone happy and I've decided to stop trying. I am who I am.

# @OBKNY

My life was pretty boring before I started using Vine. I went to school and worked. Since Instagram was the best app available at the time, I posted photos on it. I found myself checking my account constantly.

I had also been doing YouTube videos. One of my videos generated almost 900,000 views. After that, I began to make more creative videos. They all seemed to do pretty well, and I gained many subscribers to my YouTube channel. I started to collaborate with friends on skits, and we got much support and recognition online.

A friend thought that I would love Vine, and she insisted that I check it out. I instantly fell in love with it. I vined all day. I was instantly caught up in it, and I couldn't stop. I loved the fact that I could express myself, show others that I had talent, and instantly get feedback. My first vines were filmed in my room. It was my safe haven. I did voice overs, skits, and lip-syncing. I found it to be somewhat difficult to deliver something in six seconds, much less do it perfectly.

I got noticed on the app quickly, but revines didn't yet exist. I would only get a few likes per video. I was happy to get those likes, and I felt a responsibility to continue to entertain my supporters. As months went by, I found myself wanting to try something new. I wanted to push the envelope. From what I was seeing, everyone was doing comedy on their vines. I knew that there was more that could be done with the app, and I decided to change my approach.

I began to do motivational and artistic vines. People wanted comedy, but let's be realistic. Not everyone wants to laugh all the time. I thought maybe people needed uplifting messages. I had six seconds to make someone's day better, maybe even change their outlook for the day, or for their life. Why not try to do so? Today, I get so much more out of Vine. I see that it is possible to make a positive impact on someone else's life. When I get comments like "Hey, you motivate me to do better in life" it encourages me to keep going, to keep creating, and to spread more positivity. It shows me that I am making a difference.

My advice to other Viners is "Be you." Stop trying to chase Vine fame. That whole concept is stupid because if Vine were to disappear we would all just be regular people. Be original. Stop trying to gain followers. Stop trying to use other people's ideas to gain recognition. When you do those things you only appear to want attention for all the wrong reasons.

Vine has allowed me to meet so many amazing, talented people. It brings people together.

# @jeffrey marsh

The very first sound on my very first vine is "Go." It's my boyfriend's pleading voice. He wants me to perform NOW because, as you might have guessed, the six seconds were already running out.

The format of Vine made me skeptical. I couldn't possibly do anything with just six seconds! Like many things I'm uncertain about, but stick with, this app turned out to be pretty much the coolest thing ever. I've met the coolest people ever. From an outsider's perspective, Vine and I are not a very good match. I'm thirty-six, my message is uncommon, my presentation - the way I dress and speak, is light years away from anything on the Popular Page, but that's one of the beautiful things about Vine. People who need to hear your message will find it, and they will tag friends who they think need to hear your words too. Vine can be a loving community that way. While people on the app often promote racial differences or gender stereotypes, it generally has also been a connection point for me and other people who feel left out of the figurative popularity contests.

There is a dark side to an unfiltered commenting system on any app: snap judgments of the immature and mean. For every "Faggot," "Ha Gay," or even "Please commit suicide NOW" I get, there are countless numbers of "You saved my life," "I stopped cutting because of you," "Thank you," and "I'm finally proud of myself," Those positive comments make the unfortunate words of jerks seem tiny and irrelevant. Overall, Vine has been a joyous experience.

That first vine ("Go!") was an experiment. It was a few months ago and I'm still experimenting. What hasn't changed from those early vines is my desire to be a voice for those who feel left out, misunderstood, and forgotten. I grew up before positive gay images were on TV. Actually, I grew up before gay images were on TV at all. From the beginning, I have been trying to show anyone who will watch a pleasant, kind, well-adjusted (if indeed I am) gay person. I like to look pretty. I want to share that with people.
Vine is brilliant that way; there is no gatekeeper; so those who need it can do something creative that might never have worked elsewhere.

Every person who has gained a following on Vine got there through the generosity of others. We got there through the revines of others. People who already have a following share your work with their followers. My first big revine was a shock because I'm not the typical Viner. With the choice to revine me, someone might draw hate from some very vocal and bigoted Vine users. They may also lose followers, but, a very kind and courageous Viner clicked the revine button on a simple vine of mine that said, "The world needs more people who are willing to be brave and who are willing to be themselves".

My page has grown steadily since.

I would never have been able to spread this message of self-acceptance without Vine. I tried YouTube. Heck, I even tried in person! But it's this app, this stream of six-second clips that has helped me tell more than a few kids "You're not alone." It's helped me tell more than a few adults the same thing. People look at my Instagram now. People actually read my quirky, positive Tweets.

It's easy to connect with people. You just have to be honest with them.

Vine, to me, is a multi-faceted communication tool. It is a means to share bite-sized portions of humor, experiences, ideas, and dare I say it, wisdom.

Through Vine, I have made good friends with whom I may have never crossed paths. Many have inspired me, and it is my hope that my small contribution inspires them.

Before Vine, I gained a modicum of fame working as an improvisational comedic actor at various renaissance festivals in the southeastern US. I did this for a total of 20 years, and while I continue to do so, over time I came to realize that the audience for my performances was being stifled by the limited exposure that such venues provide. I knew I needed to diversify. The most sensible solution was to take things online. The character I had created, IK, King of the Trolls, was rather popular. Trolls belong on the Internet, don't they?

Accordingly, I started brainstorming ideas for various web series and whatnot, but the problem with such ideas is that they need to rely on other people and have to deal with others who lack the motivation to make things happen. One day, a good friend introduced me to Vine. I was immediately hooked.

Vine was a means of making little videos all alone when and wherever I wanted, without the need of a crew of any kind. There was a host of others who, like me, wanted to make others laugh and smile. I remember making my first couple of vines and the anticipation of when I'd be able to reveal myself in full costume. I remember the excitement I felt when people started liking and sharing and commenting.

Earlier, a humorous or philosophical thought might have come to mind and then be lost in the wind just as quickly. Now, when such thoughts come to me, I share them on Vine. As things are, I have only a handful of followers. And that suits me just fine. The only reason I'd want more followers is so that I can make more people laugh, make more people think, and inspire more minds to do more awesome things.

My small amount of fame from renaissance festivals has shown me plainly that the glory of fame is an illusion. To become famous means losing privacy, not to mention gaining the responsibility of being a role model. Most celebrities tend to not understand this. But I digress.

I eagerly await the days ahead, making vines, making friends, making smiles, and sharing wisdom.

# @Halfway House Rejects

*As written by @NorthernBeaver*

December 6, 2013. There I was, sitting in my car in the freezing cold, in a Wal Mart parking lot, talking to my phone. I was announcing the very first hash tag for the new Vine group I cofounded, and had no idea if anyone would participate.

Days earlier, I was in a chat with @Genialola, @Steph B Trippin and @Rory Rumperton, three of the funniest Viners I'd met in my fairly short time on Vine. We thought it might be fun to have a weekly hash tag event where we could goof off and act like idiots. Our tag line later became "A hash tag contest from your favorite fuckups!" All four of us had established some shady characters on Vine. Drunk Debbie, Crack head Susie, Coke head Lorraine and Pill Poppin' Pete were becoming well known in our circle of friends. We agreed on the name, Halfway House Rejects (HHR for short) and invited all of our friends to join in on the fun every Thursday (8pm EST).

At first, we didn't have any set rules or organization, we were just being silly. We realized, however, that if we wanted HHR to go anywhere, we'd have to step things up. I remembered seeing other groups who had a new face every week. We needed incentives for people to put out the effort, so we introduced having a "Guest Reject" every week, and made it into a contest. The first few weeks gave us enough practice to put together an actual organized "program" of sorts. We began asking Viners who had a lot of followers to help out by giving HHR a shout out/ contest reminder. We also noticed that a lot of Viners are musically inclined and added a musical guest feature. For lack of a better comparison, we try to have organized elements likened to SNL.

Halfway House Rejects aims to bring new faces to the game. We usually favor the underfollowed, but there have been some well-established Viners who have hosted, as well. We don't have restrictions on how many followers a potential winner may have. We've had some incredibly talented people host for us. The biggest thing we look at is creativity. If we can convince people to get off their butts, get into character and act the fool, we've done our part. Thursday nights have become like a four-hour sketch comedy show for me.

We also get a lot of support from other Viners, particularly from @Team Glory Hole. You would think that other groups might try to compete against us, but there has been nothing but love. Recently, one of my friends was part of another hash tag contest that had just begun, and their contest overlapped with HHR. Rather than draw a line in the sand, we invited each other to participate in both tags and support one another.

I can't believe the creativity that HHR has elicited from people. Sometimes I still go back to old hash tags and laugh. I've seen people make vines about how much they're looking forward to Thursday night.

Any of my fellow Rejects will tell you that I'm anal retentive. I send each new winner an email explaining the structure, their "duties", and answer any questions they may have. Many hosts treat it as though it's a very big deal; after all, they're in a spotlight of sorts. The permanent members and I want to help each host shine, to do well and hopefully gain more of a following. Sometimes I have to step back and watch it all happen. I swell with absolute pride when I see our tag trend. Best of all, we've not only made close friendships with each other, we've become close with past winners, as well.

That night outside of Wal Mart, in my car, I announced the tag, but I didn't think that we'd continue with it as long as we have. Maybe we've created a monster, but it's a damn funny one. I'm lucky that I get to be a permanent member, because many of our hosts don't want to leave! We're a good group of people, and we hope to keep the laughs coming.

# Eleven

## Your Vine Story

## *Your Vine Story*

The endings of books like these usually have some lesson to be learned. Perhaps something truly inspirational to get you through your day, something to let you know that what you've read may change your life.

We don't wish to impart that upon you. You have read enough inspiration from the people in this book. For the authors to impart any more would diminish their stories.

This is not the end of the story. *You* are the beginning of it. While this book has come to an ending does not mean Vine's story has come to an end.

Your story is continuing as we speak. Your hopes, dreams, fears, and joys are a story to be told, whether it's through Vine, Pheed, Facebook, or remembered by your loved ones.

We have plans for future works further discussing the impact social media has upon our lives. We are looking for people who wish to share their stories about the impact social media has had on their lives. If you have a story to tell, please contact us at YourVineStory@mail.com.

Go out there and make your life worth more than what social media can ever create. Remember; let social media be a great supplement to your life, not a substitute.